NO FUSS COOKING

NO FUSS COOKING

100 RECIPES YOU CAN'T GO WRONG WITH

SHEEMA & JHAMPAN MOOKERJEE

Food photographs by Ashish Chawla

VIKING

To our parents who taught us how to cook and love food.

Penguin Books India (P) Ltd., 11 Community Centre, Panchsheel Park, New Delhi 110 017, India
Penguin Books Ltd., 80 Strand, London WC2R 0RL, UK
Penguin Putnam Inc., 375 Hudson Street, New York, NY 10014, USA
Penguin Books Australia Ltd., 250 Camberwell Road, Camberwell, Victoria 3124, Australia
Penguin Books Canada Ltd., 10 Alcorn Avenue, Suite 300, Toronto, Ontario, M4V 3B2, Canada
Penguin Books (NZ) Ltd., Cnr Rosedale & Airborne Roads, Albany, Auckland, New Zealand

First published in Viking by Penguin Books India 2002

10 9 8 7 6 5 4 3 2 1

Designed by Dorling Kindersley (India) Pvt. Ltd.
Designer: Romi Chakraborty
DTP: Narender Kumar
Printed at International Print-o-Pac, Noida

contents

Paneer, Soya, Tofu

Eggs

Fish

acknowledgements

Thanks to all our friends in whose houses we've shared warm meals and imbibed food tips and recipes over the years. The names are so numerous that they cannot all be listed, but if any of you pick up this book and remember a meal shared, you've had some contribution to make in our food consciousness.

The Tomato Rice recipe comes from Sudha G. Tilak (who says her family back home in Chennai will be in splits if they hear she is being taken seriously food-wise). The Masala Bhindi comes from Jyoti Sabharwal (though out of sheer laziness we discovered the complicated stuffing process could be skipped). Another brilliant vegetarian dish, Green Pumpkin and Raw Mango, is thanks to Panditji *urf* Ajay Chaudhury.

Thanks to didi (Shoma Sen) for the Egg-drop Curry and the Ratnagiri Fish Curry; she in turn will thank her mother-in-law for them. And we owe the Bihar Fish Curry to Shanti—a household help we once had, who is now eking out a living somewhere in the interior of Jharkhand.

The lovely Strawberry Cheesecake recipe is from Malavika Talukdar who gave us the steps in the most precise and no-fuss way imaginable. She was also sweet enough to lend us her house for the photo-shoot and we created enough of a fuss in it to almost belie the claim of the book!

Another generous shoot-host was V.K. Karthika, our commissioning editor, whose brilliant idea this book was three years ago when she had dropped in for a meal. Sherna Wadia, our editor, who is yet to taste our cooking, made this book better with her eye for detail. Many more hearty meals to them and to all those who made it possible for this book to be a success.

no fuss cooking

This book is written for all those who would like to cook and eat at home, but don't do so because 'cooking is so hassly'. Some people don't cook because they don't have enough experience in the kitchen, while others flinch at the thought of fussing and sweating for hours over complicated lists of ingredients and recipes. Some feel they could do more interesting things than spend hours preparing meals like their mothers and aunts did. But the bottom line is that most people would like to cook and share a satisfying meal at home with family and friends.

In our own busy lives—juggling between work, children, socializing, and other activities—we've learnt to cut down cooking to a minimalist art. We like to call it an art because we love food too much to sacrifice taste or quality. So with each improvisation of a favourite dish, we've discovered how a step can be skipped, a procedure simplified, or a number of steps combined, to produce delicious food quite effortlessly. We love to eat and entertain and have, over the years, made cooking such a pleasurable activity that it continues to be a joy.

So join our invitation to become a no-fuss cook—one who delights in cooking, feeding and eating; does it with the least amount of sweat and toil (and oil) and revels in the joy of creating. But it cannot happen at once; prepare a dish a couple of times, sniff out the differences each time, and improve on what you made before. Any food enthusiast will tell you that recipes do not create flavour, it is the cook who does it. And if you have a problem, write to <jhampansheema@vsnl.com>.

basic ingredients

There are a few basic ingredients that you need to stock up on to prepare the recipes in this cookbook. But before we come to the lists, a few words about rice and dal.

rice

There are many varieties of rice sold in the market in various price ranges. The higher end rice is usually basmati or some local regional varieties, and are meant for special occasions, while each region also has a cheaper variety for daily use.

However, there are two standard types of rice—boiled, and polished or milled. The former is steamed before the husk is removed and retains valuable nutrients (especially of the vitamin B group). The latter is polished to make it white and like all refined products loses a lot of its natural goodness. In Hindi boiled rice is known as 'usna chaval', while the polished one is known as 'adva chaval'. These days you can also get brown or red rice, which are actually the healthiest, but also the most expensive. They take longer to cook and do not go well with all dishes.

dal

Like rice, dals also come in bewildering varieties. Unless you want to store a large variety, it should suffice to keep about three husked dals—masoor, pigeon peas (tuvar/arhar) and moong—along with any two whole varieties like moong and kidney beans (rajma).

items for the store cupboard

Spice powders (100 gms sachets):
Amchur (dry mango powder)

Black pepper powder

Chana masala (optional)

Coriander powder

Cumin powder

Garam masala powder

Kashmiri chilli powder

Sambar masala (optional)

Turmeric powder

Whole Spices (buy 50 gms, unless specified otherwise)
Ajwain

Aniseed (saunf)

Asafoetida (hing) – 10 gms

Bay leaves (tej patta) – 10 gms

Black peppercorns

Cardamom – black (badi ilaichi)

Cardamom – green (chhoti ilaichi)

Cinnamon (dal chini)

Cloves (laung)

Cumin seeds (jeera)

Dried whole red chillies

Fenugreek seeds (methi)

Mace (javitri) – 10 gms

Mustard seeds (black)

Nigella seeds (kalaunji)

Nutmeg (jaiphal) – 4 pieces

Panch phoron

Poppy seeds (khus-khus) – optional

Dal (500 gms)
Husked Bengal gram (chana dal)

Husked masoor (red lentils)

Pigeon peas (tuvar/arhar)

Husked moong

Whole moong

Whole black lentils (urad)

Kidney beans (rajma)

Chickpeas (kabuli chana)

Other items
500 gms gram flour (besan)

1 litre sunflower oil

1 litre mustard oil

500 gms ghee

2-5 kg rice

500 gms salt

2 kg sugar

5 kg wheat flour

Special items
Tomato purée

Vinegar (buy natural vinegar)

Coconut milk powder

Soy sauce

Worcestershire sauce

Tamarind

basic kitchen equipment

For a person who believes in no-fuss cookery, the kitchen should be free of clutter too. Buy utensils with a purpose—target each item for a particular use. We give below the basic equipment needed for an Indian kitchen.

Utensil	*Use*
2 kadhai—1 large (12" diameter) and 1 small (8" diameter)—with lids to size	**Cooking Indian-style dishes—dry and curried** **Deep-frying**
3-4 deep pans or dekchi in different sizes, with lids (try to avoid aluminium as its long-term use is considered to be toxic) stainless steel, preferably with a heavy copper bottom is ideal, though nowadays you also have other options of cook-and-serve or non-stick pans.	**Boiling** **Cooking rice or pasta** **Storing cut or cooked ingredients**
A medium-sized all-purpose saucepan with lid	**Making tea, coffee, etc** **Boiling small quantities of liquid**
A saucepan or deep pan with lid reserved only for milk	**Boiling and storing milk**
2 non-stick frying pans with lids—12" and 8"diameters	**Shallow/deep frying**
A tempering pan (see pg.7)	**Seasoning food**
Spoons, ladles and spatulas of various shapes and sizes to suit you	
A pair of pincers (pakad)	**For handling hot pans**
Knives of various sizes—serrated and plain	

Utensil	*Use*
A large plastic strainer or a stainless steel colander	**Draining rice and pasta** **Washing and draining cut vegetables**
A small strainer	**Straining tea**
A tava (iron griddle)	**Making roti** **Dry-roasting spices**
Rolling board and pin	**Making roti, poori, paratha**
Chopping board	**Chopping ingredients**
Grater	**Grating onion, ginger and other vegetables as well as cheese, lime rind, nutmeg, etc.**
Potato peeler	**Peeling vegetables**
Mortar and pestle (metal or stone)	**Pounding small quantities of spices**
Electric blender/grinder or food processor	**Heavy wet and dry grinding, puréeing, liquidizing, etc.**

table of measures

The cup measure used in this book is 225 ml (8-oz)

1 tsp = 5 ml

1 tbsp = 3 tsp

A pinch = 1/8 tsp (literally a pinch)

A dash = 1-2 drops

All spoon measures are level

basic techniques

Using a Pressure Cooker

- Place the ingredients in the cooker with water to cover (or according to the recipe) and close the lid with the weight on the pressure valve.
- Place the cooker over high heat and allow the first whistle to go off.
- Lower heat and keep the cooker over low heat for the time specified.

Some clarifications:

- A common mistake is to pressure-cook food over high heat and time the cooking period according to the number of whistles. This is an inaccurate way of fixing your cooking time and tends to overcook food.
- Some pressure cooker manuals recommend that you fit on the weight after the steam emerges from the outlet. This additional step is not really necessary.

Warning: While washing your pressure cooker do take off the weight and see to it that the outlet for steam is never clogged with grime.

Steaming

This is an oil-free cooking process that retains the nutrients in the food to the maximum (unlike boiling). To steam, place the ingredients in a tightly closed steel or aluminium container (or cover the container with foil). Bring 2-3 cups water to boil in a deep pan or kadhai over high heat, and place the container in the centre. Cover the outer vessel and place a heavy weight over the cover. Steam the food for the time specified in the recipe. Alternatively, place the closed container in a rice cooker containing 2-3 cups water, and steam.

Tempering (Seasoning in Hot Oil)

An essential part of Indian cooking is aromatising food by frying whole spices in hot oil or ghee, and adding it to the dish. This process is known variously in different parts of the country as tadka, baghar, phodni, phoron, etc.

Tempering may be done at the end of cooking, where the hot oil and spices are poured over the completed dish, or at the start, where the spices are first seared in hot oil and the remaining ingredients are then added and cooked.

Where the spices are poured over the finished dish, tempering is best done in a small utensil with a thick base. Specific pans are available in the market for this. We refer to it as the 'tempering pan' in this book. Since the pan gets very hot, it is convenient to have one with a handle. Otherwise use a pincer or 'pakad' to grip the pan—avoid a duster as you might burn your hands.

Where you do the tempering first and then add the remaining ingredients, you will of course use a large pan, preferably a kadhai, in which the dish is to be cooked, or the pressure cooker, if you are going to pressure-cook the food.

Adding Chillies to the Tempering

When using whole chillies (fresh or dried) in the tempering, break the tops of the chillies. This allows the hot air inside to escape, otherwise the chilli will explode. Similarly, split open the skin of a cardamom before adding it to hot oil.

Wet-grinding

Many Indian dishes need a thick wet masala base that was traditionally ground by hand on a stone. Nowadays this is easily done in a mixer. The standard Indian mixer has a jug-like blender or liquidizer, and a smaller spice/chutney grinder. If you are grinding more than a cup of masala, use the blender. For quantities less than that use the spice/chutney grinder.

The standard wet masala paste consists of ginger-garlic-onion, or each of these ground separately. Onions and ginger need to be peeled and roughly chopped before grinding, while garlic cloves can be put into the mixer whole, after peeling. It is a good idea to make enough ginger-garlic-onion paste for a week at a time and store it in the fridge in a closed container.

For a cup of paste you will need 3 medium onions, 2" piece ginger and 1 whole head of garlic. Peel and prepare these and put into the blender with 2 tbsp water. Start by running the machine on slow speed and gradually increase it to medium and then high, to make a smooth paste. If the ingredients don't circulate, give them a stir, add 2 tbsp of water and grind.

Wet masala pastes of other spices and herbs can be made in the same way. Each mixer comes with an instruction booklet and you should follow the procedure described for your gadget.

Note: Mustard and poppy seed are two spices that do not grind in the mixer if you add water to them. Sometimes a recipe may call for wet mustard or poppy seed paste. First dry-grind the spice into a fine powder and then stir in water by the teaspoonful to make a thick paste.

Dry-grinding

In India it is the norm to buy turmeric, red chilli, coriander and cumin powders ready-made from the grocers. However, you may sometimes need a special ground spice such as mustard, cinnamon or aniseed. In that case, put the whole spice into the spice grinder and grind without water till it is a fine powder.

Making Bean/Moong Sprouts

Ideally moong sprouts are made in an earthenware or ceramic bowl, so that they can 'breathe'. For 2 cups of sprouts, soak 1 cup whole moong in 2 cups water overnight. In the morning, drain the water out and cover the top of the bowl with a thick napkin that has been dipped in water and wrung out. Place the bowl in a warm corner of the kitchen. Sprinkle some water over the napkin at the end of the day. Leave to sprout for two days, repeating the watering routine each morning and night. For Chinese-style sprouts, with roots that are at least 1-2" long, leave to germinate for 3-4 nights.

Hung Curd

This is a magic ingredient that can be put to many uses in the kitchen. Fresh curd is tied up in a porous cotton cloth and hung over the sink for the water to drip out. The longer you hang it the drier the curd gets, thus lending itself to different uses. Given below is a table that gives the approximate hanging time for use in different preparations. The amount of curd used is 2 cups.

No of hours	*Preparation*
1/2	Raita, marinades, souring agent for meats
1	Salad dressing, substitute for mayonnaise
3-4	Sandwich spread
5-6	Desserts such as shrikhand, cheese-cake

Tamarind Paste

For 4 tbsp tamarind paste, soak a lime-sized ball of tamarind in ½ cup hot water for 30 minutes. Mash the tamarind and strain the juice out through a strainer. You can also buy packaged tamarind paste which is an equally good substitute.

Grated/Ground Coconut

You can grate or grind coconut in the blender. Prise the coconut out of its shell, peel off the brown skin with a potato peeler and cut the coconut into 2-3" pieces. Put these pieces in the blender and grind with the mincing blade to the desired consistency.

Coconut Milk

For 1 cup thick milk, grate or grind the flesh of one coconut as described above. Pour in 1 cup boiling water into the coconut and stir. Strain out the milk through a strainer. You may add one more cup of boiling water to the coconut and strain out thin coconut milk, for second-time use. Coconut milk in tetra packs or coconut milk powder in sachets make a good substitute.

soups

A hot and nourishing soup can make a fantastic start to a meal or can even be a meal in itself. Soups are a good way of serving the family vegetables in a disguised form. They are wonderful for the sick and convalescing or for tired souls who don't want to cook up a full meal at the end of the day. In India we tend to think of soups only in winter. But there are a few chilled soups in this chapter to restore heated tempers in the warm season.

ONE-OF-EACH SOUP

Serves: 6

This name comes from the fact that just one of each vegetable is used, resulting in a delicious winter soup. You can vary the vegetables according to availability, but see that you always have the onion and tomato for taste.

1 large carrot, scraped and roughly chopped

1 large potato, peeled and roughly chopped

1 turnip, scraped and roughly chopped

1 beetroot, scraped and roughly chopped

1 medium onion, quartered

1 large, ripe tomato, roughly chopped

1 small cabbage, chopped

1 stalk celery or a small bunch coriander leaves, chopped

1 tsp salt

1/2 tsp black pepper powder

- Place all ingredients in a pressure cooker with 6 cups water and cook under pressure for 5 minutes.
- Open cooker after it has cooled.
- Allow vegetables to cool a little and blend to a purée in a liquidizer, or pass through a large metal strainer.
- Adjust water and seasoning.
- Serve piping hot with buttered rolls.

CAULIFLOWER AND BROCCOLI SOUP

Serves: 6

You may make this soup with only cauliflower, or both the vegetables, which complement each other well.

1 small cauliflower, (250 gms), roughly chopped and washed

250 gms broccoli, roughly chopped and washed

2 cups toned milk

1 tsp salt

1/2 tsp black pepper powder

1/2 cup fresh cream (optional)

- Place vegetables in a pressure cooker with 2 cups water and cook under pressure for 2 minutes.
- Open cooker after it has cooled.
- Allow vegetables to cool a little and blend with milk to a purée in a liquidizer.
- Adjust consistency of soup with more milk or hot water, if required.
- Add salt and pepper, and adjust seasoning.
- Those who are not counting calories can serve it with fresh cream stirred in.

SPINACH SOUP

Serves: 6

This is another simple-to-make soup. Nutmeg is a spice that seems to be made for spinach. Please don't skip it. You can buy it at any grocery store.

500 gms spinach

2 cups milk

1/2 tsp grated nutmeg

1 tsp salt

1/2 tsp black pepper powder

2 tbsp fresh cream

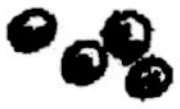

- Clean spinach, discarding dried, yellow or worm-eaten leaves. If the stalks are tough (they do not snap off easily when you bend them), discard.
- Wash at least twice in a large basin with plenty of water.
- Place spinach in a pressure cooker with 2 cups water, close cooker and place over heat. Remove from heat as soon as cooker reaches full pressure (first whistle).
- Place cooker immediately under running cold water to reduce pressure and open. (This retains the fresh green colour of the spinach.)
- Allow spinach to cool and blend to a purée in a liquidizer, with milk.
- Heat soup and add nutmeg, salt and pepper. Adjust seasoning and stir in cream.
- Serve hot.

Cook's tip: The cream removes any bitter taste that the spinach might have.

CHICKEN AND SWEET CORN SOUP

Serves: 6

1/2 kg chicken or bony parts like neck, wings, rib-cage

1 tin (400 gms) creamed sweet corn

1 tsp salt

1/2 tsp black pepper powder

2 eggs, lightly beaten

To serve

1/4 cup soy sauce

5-6 green chillies, finely chopped (optional)

- Pressure-cook chicken with 4 cups water for 5 minutes.
- Cool and strain stock. De-bone chicken and add flesh to stock.
- Stir in sweet corn and add water to make 6 cups of soup.
- Add salt and pepper, and bring to boil over medium heat.
- Gently pour eggs into boiling soup through a large-holed strainer or slotted spoon. Keep stirring soup till eggs are set.
- Combine green chillies (if used) with soy sauce and serve in a separate bowl to have with soup.

CURRIED CARROT SOUP

Serves: 6

8 medium carrots (500 gms), scraped and diced

2 chicken or vegetable stock cubes

1 cup thick coconut milk or 1/2 cup cream

1 tsp sambar masala powder

1 tsp salt

1/2 tsp black pepper powder

Lime juice as required

Garnish

1 lime, cut in slices

2 tbsp chopped coriander leaves

- Place carrots with 3 cups water in a pan and bring to boil. Lower heat and simmer till soft.
- Allow to cool, combine with remaining ingredients except garnish and blend to a purée in a liquidizer. You may also press the carrots through a strainer to purée them.
- Place puréed soup in a pan and simmer over low heat for 5 minutes.
- Serve in individual bowls with a squeeze of lime and garnished with a slice of lime and coriander leaves.

COLD CUCUMBER SOUP

Serves: 6

3 medium cucumbers (250 gms)

2 chicken or vegetable stock cubes

1 cup curd, whipped well

1 tsp salt

1/2 tsp black pepper powder

Lime juice as required

Garnish

1 lime, cut in slices

2 tbsp chopped coriander leaves

- Peel and grate cucumber. Taste to see if bitter before using.
- Dissolve stock cubes in 2 cups warm water.
- Combine all ingredients except garnish and blend in a liquidizer. You may also just stir the ingredients together.
- Chill in the refrigerator for 1-2 hours.
- Serve in individual bowls with a squeeze of lime and garnished with a slice of lime and coriander leaves.

CLEAR CHICKEN SOUP

Serves: 4-6

1/2 kg chicken or bony parts like neck, wings, rib-cage

1 tsp salt

1/2 tsp black pepper powder

1 stalk celery with leaves, washed and roughly chopped

2 spring onions with greens, finely chopped

2 tbsp finely julienned cabbage

1 small carrot, finely julienned

1 tbsp soy sauce (optional)

- Place chicken with 4 cups water, salt, pepper and celery in a pressure cooker and cook under pressure for 5 minutes.
- Open cooker after it has cooled.
- Strain stock and return to pressure cooker.
- Remove flesh from chicken and add 2-3 tbsp to stock. Use remaining chicken flesh for sandwiches or Chinese fried rice (see p. xxx).
- Bring stock to boil over high heat, add spring onions, cabbage and carrot, and cook uncovered for exactly a minute.
- Stir in soy sauce (if used) and serve piping hot.

EASY TOM YAM SOUP

Serves: 4

1/2 kg chicken or bony parts like neck, wings, rib-cage

200 gms fresh or frozen prawns, any size, shelled, de-veined and washed

1 tsp salt

1/2 tsp black pepper powder

2 lemon-flavoured stock cubes

Juice of 1 lime

2 tbsp chopped coriander leaves

3-4 green chillies, finely chopped

- Place chicken with 4 cups water in a pressure cooker and cook under pressure for 5 minutes.
- Open cooker after it has cooled.
- Strain stock, add prawns and boil for 5 minutes.
- Stir in remaining ingredients and serve hot.

Cook's tip: You can de-bone the chicken and use the flesh for sandwiches or a salad.

rice

There are innumerable varieties of rice available in India, and cooking any one to absolute perfection needs experience and practice. Each variety requires a slightly different quantity of water and cooking time. So, whenever you cook a variety or brand of rice that you have not used before, follow the basic procedure given below and adjust the water and cooking time till it is just right.

PLAIN RICE

Serves: 2

The standard proportion for cooking rice is 1 cup of rice to 2 cups of water. To test if the rice is done, press a grain between your thumb and finger. If it is still hard and the water has dried up, add an additional ½ cup water, cover and cook further till tender. If you are using a pressure cooker, and the rice is not cooked when you open the cooker, add the additional water, cover lightly and complete the cooking without pressure.

Before cooking, put rice in a broad flat pan and check for stones and other impurities. If you buy it from a large grocery store, this is often not necessary. Then wash rice, changing the water thrice.

1 cup rice, cleaned and washed

2 cups water

Cooking Rice in a Pan

- Place rice and water in a deep pan that has a lid.
- Cook over high heat till water comes to boil.
- Lower heat and cover pan partially, leaving a slight opening to let the steam escape, or the water will bubble over.

- Keep checking to see if water is absorbed totally. Once this is done, turn off heat and cover pan completely. Let the rice cook a little longer, around 5 minutes, in its own steam.

Cooking Rice in a Pressure Cooker

- Place the rice and water in a pressure cooker. Close cooker, put the weight on the pressure valve and place over high heat till steam starts hissing from the pressure valve. (This is the stage just before the cooker reaches full pressure and the first whistle goes off.) Turn off heat and open the cooker after it has cooled.
- The rice continues to cook in its own steam even when the heat has been turned off.

GHEE BHAAT

Serves: 4

This deliciously fragrant and light dish goes well with any vegetable, chicken or mutton curry to make a very special meal.

2 cups basmati rice, cleaned and washed

1/2 tsp salt

2 tbsp pure ghee

2 bay leaves (tej patta)

1/2 tsp cumin seeds

2 x 1" sticks cinnamon

4-6 green cardamoms

1/2 cup shelled green peas, boiled (optional)

- Cook rice as given for plain rice (see p. xx), adding salt to the water before cooking it.
- Place ghee in a tempering pan over medium heat, till just melted.
- Add bay leaves and fry for 15 seconds.
- Sprinkle in cumin seeds and when they start sputtering, add cinnamon and cardamoms.
- Fry for 30 seconds and pour contents of pan over rice.
- Add green peas (if used).
- Stir rice well to mix thoroughly.

CURD RICE

Serves: 2

2 cups cooked rice (you may use leftover rice)

2 cups curd, beaten till smooth

1/2 tsp salt

Tempering

2 tsp oil

2-3 whole dried red chillies, tops broken

1/2 tsp husked black lentils (urad dal)

1/2 tsp mustard seeds

2 sprigs curry leaves

- Bring rice to room temperature.
- Mix curd with salt and stir into rice.
- Place oil in a tempering pan over medium heat, till just beginning to smoke.
- Add red chillies and fry for 15 seconds.
- Add dal and fry till light brown.
- Sprinkle in mustard seeds and fry till they start to sputter. Do not allow dal to burn. If the oil is getting too hot, turn heat down or remove pan from heat.
- Add curry leaves and immediately pour contents of pan over rice.
- Stir well and serve with pickles and papad.

CHINESE FRIED RICE

Serves: 4

2 cups rice, cleaned and washed

2 tbsp oil

1/2 tsp finely minced garlic

1/2 tsp finely minced ginger

1 carrot, scraped and cut into juliennes

10 French beans, ends trimmed and finely sliced

1/2 cup shelled green peas and/or finely sliced button mushrooms

2 spring onions with greens, finely chopped

2 eggs and/or 100 gms ham, chopped and/or 100 gms shelled shrimps, de-veined, washed and boiled

1 tsp salt

1/2 tsp black pepper powder

2 tbsp soy sauce

- Cook rice as given for plain rice (see p. xxx).
- Place oil in a large pan or kadhai over medium heat, till just beginning to smoke.
- Add garlic and ginger and stir-fry for 15 seconds.
- Raise heat to high and add vegetables in the order given, so that you begin with the ones that need more cooking. Stir-fry for a minute each, over high heat, before adding the next.
- Add eggs (if used) and stir fast till they scramble. Add ham and/or shrimps (if used) and stir-fry for 1-2 minutes further.
- Lower heat and mix in salt, pepper and then rice.
- Sprinkle in soy sauce and stir well.
- Continue cooking and stirring over low heat, till rice is completely coated with sauce and turns light brown.

TOMATO RICE

Serves: 2-3

2 tbsp oil

A pinch powdered asafoetida (hing)

1/4 tsp husked black lentils (urad dal)

1/2 tsp mustard seeds

2-3 sprigs curry leaves

4-5 medium, ripe tomatoes (250 gms), very finely chopped

1 tsp salt

2 tsp sambar masala powder

2 cups cooked rice (you may use leftover rice)

Garnish
2 tbsp chopped coriander leaves

- Place oil in a large kadhai over medium heat, till just beginning to smoke.
- Sprinkle in asafoetida and dal, and keep stirring till dal is light brown.
- Add mustard seeds and curry leaves, and when mustard seeds start to sputter, add tomatoes, salt and sambar masala.
- Cook for 5-7 minutes, till tomatoes are reduced to half the original quantity.
- Add rice and mix well.
- Garnish with coriander leaves and serve on its own with papad, or with a light vegetable dish.

LEMON OR LIME RICE

Serves: 2-3

2 cups cooked rice (you may use leftover rice)

Juice of 1/2 lemon or 1 lime

3/4 tsp salt

Tempering

1 tsp oil

2 whole dried red chillies, tops broken

A pinch powdered asafoetida (hing)

1/2 tsp husked black lentils (urad dal)

1/2 tsp mustard seeds

2 sprigs curry leaves

1/2 tsp turmeric powder

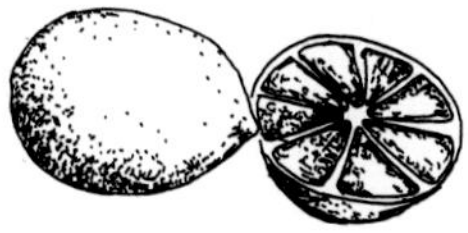

- Bring rice to room temperature.
- Place oil in a tempering pan over medium heat, till just beginning to smoke.
- Add red chillies and asafoetida, and fry for 5 seconds.
- Add dal and fry till light brown.
- Sprinkle in mustard seeds and when they start to sputter, add curry leaves and turmeric.
- Almost immediately, remove from heat and pour contents of pan over rice.
- Stir in lemon or lime juice and salt, and mix till well blended.

dal

Dal is a universal food in India and is usually a must for most meals. Dal-roti, dal-bhaat, parappu-sadam, are all colloquial expressions that stand for daily food. A dal can be very simple, cooked in less than 15 minutes; or complex, cooked over low heat for hours, with an array of spices. We've selected a few basic but tasty dals from all over India, but it's just a drop in the ocean.

BASIC DAL

Serves: 6

The basic method of making a dal is to cook it in a pressure cooker and then pour a tempering over it. The tempering for dal is best done in pure ghee. However, you can also use oil. If the tempering involves onions, and you need a little more cooking medium to fry it, you can avoid the ghee and use oil. Generally, 1 cup of uncooked dal suffices for 6 people, but a lot depends on how thin or thick you want the dish. Go by the following technique to cook dal.

1 cup dal

3 cups water

1 tsp salt

1/2 tsp turmeric powder (optional)

- Pick through and wash dal as given for rice (see p. 20).
- Place dal, water, salt and turmeric (if used) in a pressure cooker and cook under pressure.
- Husked Bengal gram (chana dal) needs to be cooked for 10 minutes, while the other husked dals need just 2 minutes. Whole black lentils (urad) and whole masoor need 10 minutes. The urad needs to be soaked overnight.
- Open cooker after it has cooled. The steam inside the cooker softens the dal further to the correct texture.
- Normally you shouldn't have to add any more water, but you can adjust the consistency if needed, at this stage.
- Prepare a tempering and pour it into the dal. Simmer for a few minutes and it is ready.

Tempering for husked masoor (red lentils) – I

2 tbsp ghee

2-3 whole dried red chillies, tops broken (optional)

1/2 tsp cumin seeds

1 medium onion, finely chopped

2 tbsp chopped coriander leaves (optional)

4-5 whole green chillies, tops broken

- Place ghee in a tempering pan over medium heat, till just melted.
- Add red chillies (if used) and fry till they darken slightly.
- Sprinkle in cumin seeds and fry for 5 seconds.
- Add onion and fry till golden-brown, stirring frequently. Lower heat if it starts to burn.
- Pour contents of pan over boiled dal and add coriander leaves and green chillies.
- Place dal over high heat, bring to boil, lower heat and simmer for 1-2 minutes.

Tempering for husked masoor (red lentils) – II

1 tbsp ghee

2 whole dried red chillies, tops broken

1/2 tsp nigella seeds (kalaunji)

2 tbsp chopped coriander leaves (optional)

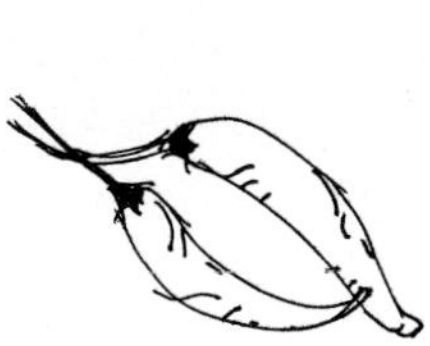

- Place ghee in a tempering pan over medium heat, till just melted. Add red chillies and fry till they darken.
- Rub nigella between your palms and sprinkle into pan.
- After 2 seconds pour contents of pan over boiled dal and mix in coriander leaves.
- Place dal over high heat, bring to boil, lower heat and simmer for 2-3 minutes.

Variations: Substitute fenugreek seeds (methi) for nigella seeds. Ensure that the spices don't burn, else the dal will be bitter.

Add 2 chopped tomatoes to dal while boiling it and use panch-phoran instead of nigella seeds.

Tempering for pigeon peas (arhar/tuvar) – I

1 tsp ghee

2 whole dried red chillies, tops broken

A pinch powdered asafoetida (hing)

1/2 tsp cumin seeds

- Place ghee in a tempering pan over medium heat, till just melted.
- Add red chillies and fry till they darken slightly.
- Add asafoetida and cumin seeds, and fry for 1-2 seconds.
- Pour contents of pan over boiled dal.
- Place dal over high heat, bring to boil, lower heat and simmer for 3-4 minutes.

Cook's tip: You may add 1/2 tsp sugar to this dal while cooking it in the pressure cooker, and beat it with an eggbeater to give it a smooth consistency.

Variation: Substitute aniseed (saunf) or ajwain in place of cumin seeds.

Tempering for pigeon peas (arhar/tuvar) – II

1 tbsp ghee

1/2 tsp mustard seeds

4-5 cloves garlic, diced

10-12 curry leaves (optional)

- Place ghee in a tempering pan over medium heat, till just melted.
- Sprinkle in mustard seeds and when they start to sputter, add garlic and fry till light brown.
- Add curry leaves and immediately pour contents of pan over boiled dal.
- Place dal over high heat, bring to boil, lower heat and simmer for 2-3 minutes.

Tempering for husked moong – I

2 tbsp ghee

2 whole dried red chillies, tops broken (optional)

1/2 tsp cumin seeds

1/2" piece ginger, cut in fine juliennes

3-4 cloves garlic, finely chopped

1 small onion, finely chopped

2 tbsp chopped coriander leaves

- Place ghee in a tempering pan over medium heat, till just melted.
- Add red chillies and cumin seeds.
- When cumin seeds start to sputter, add ginger and garlic and stir-fry for 15-30 seconds.
- Add onion and fry till golden, stirring frequently. Lower heat if it appears to be burning.
- Pour contents of pan over boiled dal and stir in coriander leaves.
- Place dal over high heat, bring to boil, lower heat and simmer for 3-4 minutes.

Tempering for husked moong – II

1 tbsp ghee

2 whole dried red chillies, tops broken

2 bay leaves (tej patta)

1/2 tsp cumin seeds

1 tsp grated ginger

4-5 whole green chillies, tops broken (optional)

1/2 tsp sugar (optional)

- Place ghee in a tempering pan over medium heat, till just melted. Add red chillies and bay leaves, and fry till they darken slightly.
- Sprinkle in cumin seeds and when they start to sputter, add ginger and stir-fry for 15 seconds.
- Pour contents of pan over boiled dal. Place dal over high heat and bring to boil.
- Add green chillies and sugar (if used), stir well, lower heat and simmer for 2-3 minutes.

SABUT MOONG

Whole Moong

Serves: 6

1 cup whole moong

1 tsp salt

1/2 tsp red chilli powder (optional)

1 tbsp chopped ginger

Tempering

1 tbsp ghee

2 medium onions, chopped

2 tsp chopped garlic

2 medium tomatoes, roughly chopped

1 tsp garam masala powder

1/2 tsp black pepper powder

Garnish

1 tbsp dried fenugreek leaves (kasuri methi) – optional

- Cook dal with salt, chilli powder, ginger and 4 cups water under pressure for 10 minutes, as given in the basic recipe for dal (see p. 28).
- Open cooker after it has cooled.
- Place ghee in a medium-sized pan over medium heat, till just melted.
- Add onions and fry till pink, stirring frequently.
- Stir in garlic, tomatoes, garam masala and pepper.
- Stir-fry till tomatoes soften and pour contents of pan into dal.
- Stir till well mixed, simmer for 3-4 minutes and serve sprinkled with dried fenugreek leaves (if used).

Cook's tip: This dal is usually eaten thick but you may add some water if you want it thin.

SABUT MASOOR

Whole Red Lentils

Serves: 6

1 cup whole masoor

1/2 tsp turmeric powder

1 tsp salt

Tempering

2 tbsp ghee

2 large onions, sliced

1 tbsp julienned ginger

6-7 cloves garlic, coarsely crushed

3-4 green chillies, chopped (optional)

1 tsp garam masala powder (optional)

2 medium tomatoes, sliced

Garnish

1 tbsp chopped coriander leaves

- Cook dal with turmeric and salt under pressure for 10 minutes, as given in the basic recipe for dal (see p. 28).
- Open cooker after it has cooled.
- Add water, if you want to thin it down, or boil to thicken to the consistency you like.
- Place ghee in a medium-sized pan over medium heat, till just melted.
- Add onions and fry till pink, stirring frequently.
- Add ginger and garlic, and stir for a few minutes till browned.
- Stir in green chillies (if used).
- Almost immediately add garam masala (if used) and tomatoes, and stir-fry on high heat for a few minutes.
- Pour contents of pan into dal, bring to boil, lower heat and simmer for 2-3 minutes.
- Serve garnished with coriander leaves.

SONA MOONG

Roasted Husked Moong with Vegetables

Serves: 6

1 cup husked moong

1/2 tsp turmeric powder

1 tsp salt

1 tbsp ginger paste

250 gms spinach, washed and chopped

2 medium carrots, peeled and cut into large pieces

1/2 cup shelled green peas, preferably fresh

4-5 whole green chillies, tops broken

Tempering

1 tsp ghee

1/2 tsp cumin seeds

2 bay leaves (tej patta)

- Clean dal and dry-roast it in a kadhai over low heat. Keep stirring till it is evenly golden-brown and exudes a roasted aroma. Allow to cool, then wash dal.
- Cook with turmeric, salt and ginger under pressure for 7 minutes, as given in the basic recipe for dal (see p. 28). (Since the dal has been roasted, it will take a little longer to cook.)
- Add water if too thick or boil down if too thin to give a medium-thick consistency. Place cooker on heat and bring dal to boil.
- Add vegetables and green chillies. Bring to boil again, cover loosely with the lid, lower heat and simmer till vegetables are done. If you are in a hurry, close cooker and cook just till it attains full pressure. Allow to cool on its own before opening.
- Place ghee in a tempering pan over medium heat, till just melted.
- Add cumin seeds and bay leaves, and when cumin seeds start to sputter, pour contents of pan into dal.
- Bring to boil, remove from heat and serve with rice to produce a complete meal.

Cook's tip: This dal can be cooked with a single vegetable or any combination. Bengalis traditionally cook it with only green peas. But there are no rules limiting the variations. It goes well with cauliflower, cabbage, bottle gourd (lauki) and any beans, like French beans, sheet beans (saem phalli), etc.

SPROUTED MOONG

Serves: 4

2 tbsp oil

2 whole dried red chillies, tops broken

1 tsp mustard seeds

10 curry leaves

1 medium onion, chopped

1 tsp chopped garlic

1 tsp chopped ginger

1 cup sprouted moong (see p. 9)

1/2 tsp salt

1/2 tsp turmeric powder

Garnish

2 tbsp freshly grated coconut (optional)

2 tbsp chopped coriander leaves (optional)

- Place oil in a pan over medium heat, till just beginning to smoke.
- Add red chillies, mustard seeds and curry leaves.
- When mustard seeds start to sputter, add onion, garlic and ginger, and fry till onion is light brown, stirring frequently. Lower heat if it appears to be burning.
- Gently add sprouts, salt and turmeric, and stir for a few minutes, sprinkling in a little water occasionally.
- Keep sprouts slightly underdone and green. Don't cook for more than 3-4 minutes.
- Garnish with coconut and coriander leaves for a special touch.

OIL-FREE KIDNEY BEANS

Rajma

Serves: 6

$1\frac{1}{2}$ cups kidney beans (rajma)

1 medium onion, chopped

1 tsp finely chopped garlic

1 tsp finely chopped ginger

2 tbsp coriander powder

2 medium tomatoes, cut into large pieces or $\frac{1}{2}$ cup tomato purée

1 tsp black pepper powder

1 tsp garam masala powder

1 tsp salt

Garnish
2 tbsp chopped coriander leaves

- Clean and wash kidney beans and soak in water for at least 6 hours or overnight.
- Rinse kidney beans well and pressure-cook for 15 minutes with 4 cups water. Open cooker after it has cooled.
- Add remaining ingredients except garnish.
- Simmer for 15 minutes over low heat, without pressure, adding water to adjust your gravy. When ready, the gravy should be thick and sticky.
- Garnish with coriander leaves before serving.

Variation: You can also cook chickpeas (kabuli chana) in the same way.

CONTINENTAL-STYLE KIDNEY BEANS

Rajma

Serves: 4-6

1 cup kidney beans (rajma)

2 tbsp oil

1 medium onion, chopped

1 tsp finely chopped garlic

1 tsp finely chopped ginger

2 stalks celery, chopped or 2 medium capsicums, de-seeded and cut into 3" pieces

1 packet (200 gms) button mushrooms, halved

2 carrots, peeled and diced

2 medium tomatoes, chopped into 6 pieces each, or 1/2 cup tomato purée

1/2 tsp black pepper powder

1 tsp salt

- Clean and wash kidney beans and soak in water for at least 6 hours, or overnight.
- Rinse well and pressure-cook with 3 cups water for 15 minutes. Open cooker after it has cooled.
- Place oil in a kadhai over medium heat, till just beginning to smoke.
- Add onion, garlic and ginger, and sauté till onion is pink, stirring frequently.
- Add celery or capsicum, mushrooms and carrots, and sauté for 2 minutes.
- Stir in tomatoes or tomato purée, pepper and salt, and cook for 5 minutes over medium heat.
- Pour in beans, add water to adjust your gravy, bring to boil, lower heat and simmer for 5 minutes.
- The gravy should be thick.
- Serve with bread or roti.

CHANA AUR LAUKI

Bengal Gram with Bottle Gourd

Serves: 4-6

1 cup husked Bengal gram (chana dal)

1 tsp salt

1/2 tsp turmeric powder

2 medium tomatoes, chopped

250 gms bottle gourd (lauki), peeled and cut into 1/2" cubes

Tempering

2 tsp ghee

A pinch powdered asafoetida (hing)

1 bay leaf

1/2 tsp cumin seeds

1" stick cinnamon

2 green cardamoms

3 cloves

- Cook dal with salt, turmeric, tomatoes and 3 cups water, under pressure for 8 minutes, as given in the basic recipe for dal (see p. 28). Allow cooker to cool on its own before opening.
- Add bottle gourd and cook under pressure for a further 2 minutes. Open cooker after it has cooled.
- Place ghee in a tempering pan over medium heat, till just melted.
- Sprinkle in asafoetida and almost immediately add remaining ingredients.
- As the whole spices release their aroma, pour contents of pan over boiled dal.
- Place cooker with dal over high heat and bring to boil, without pressure.
- Lower heat and simmer for 2-3 minutes.

Cook's tip: This makes a nutritious and tasty meal in itself, and is a good way to feed vegetables like spinach, bottle gourd, etc. to unwilling kids.

Variation: You can cook the dal with 2 cups chopped spinach in place of bottle gourd.

LIME RASAM

Serves: 4-6

$^1/_2$ cup pigeon peas (arhar/tuvar)

1 tsp salt

$^1/_2$ tsp turmeric powder

A pinch powdered asafoetida (hing)

4-5 whole green chillies, tops broken

Juice of 1-2 limes

Tempering
1 tsp oil

2-3 whole dried red chillies, tops broken

10 curry leaves

$^1/_2$ tsp mustard seeds

Garnish
2 tbsp finely chopped coriander leaves

- Cook dal with 4 cups water, salt, turmeric and asafoetida under pressure for 5 minutes, till very soft as given in the basic recipe for dal (see p. 28).
- Open cooker after it has cooled.
- Add green chillies, bring to boil, without pressure, lower heat and simmer for 5-10 minutes.
- Remove from heat and pour in lime juice.
- Place oil in a tempering pan over medium heat, till just beginning to smoke.
- Add red chillies, curry leaves and mustard seeds.
- When mustard seeds start to sputter, pour contents of pan over rasam.
- Garnish with coriander leaves and serve piping hot with rice, papad and ghee.

SAMBAR

Serves: 4-6

A wholesome sambar with your choice of vegetables makes a wonderful balanced dish. You have the protein from the dal, the vitamins from the vegetables and tamarind, and the digestive goodness of asafoetida. Use your favourite combination of vegetables—diced aubergine (baingan), pumpkin and okra (bhindi); or carrots and beans; or even just chopped spinach.

1 cup pigeon peas (arhar/tuvar)

1 heaped tsp salt

1 tsp turmeric powder

1/2 tsp sugar or jaggery

A pinch powdered asafoetida (hing)

1 tbsp sambar masala powder

2 cups diced vegetables of your choice

2 tbsp tamarind paste

Tempering

1 tsp ghee

2 whole dried red chillies, tops broken

1/2 tsp mustard seeds

10 curry leaves

- Cook dal with salt, turmeric, sugar or jaggery and 3 cups water under pressure for 3 minutes, as given in the basic recipe (see p. 28).
- Open cooker after it has cooled, add 2 cups water and bring to boil.
- Add asafoetida and sambar masala, stir well, lower heat and simmer for 5 minutes further.
- Add vegetables and cook till tender.
- Stir in tamarind paste and remove from heat.
- Place ghee in a tempering pan over medium heat, till just melted.
- Add red chillies, mustard seeds and curry leaves.
- When mustard seeds start to sputter, pour contents of pan over sambar and simmer for 3-4 minutes.
- Sambar is best served with rice and papad, or idli or dosa.

Cook's tip: If you are using okra, you might want to fry it till brown in a little oil to take away the sliminess, before adding it.

vegetables

Everyone acknowledges that a wide variety of vegetables in one's diet is the best way to get one's vitamin and mineral intake. In India we still have the privilege of being able to shop for fresh seasonal vegetables at every street corner, and thankfully the canned culture has not yet taken over. With a strong bias towards vegetarianism in many parts of our country, the repertoire of vegetable dishes is limitless. The dishes presented here are among the simplest of preparations, where just the addition of a few spices perks up the taste and yet retains the natural flavours of the vegetables.

TINDA TAMATAR

Indian Squash with Tomatoes

Serves: 4

300 gms tender seedless tinda

3 tbsp oil

3-4 green chillies, finely chopped

3 medium, ripe tomatoes, chopped

1/2 tsp turmeric powder

1 tsp salt

3 tbsp chopped coriander leaves

- You do not need to peel tinda. Slice off the ends, halve each tinda and cut into 1/2" thick slices.
- Place oil in a kadhai over medium heat, till just beginning to smoke.
- Add green chillies and almost immediately add tinda, and sauté for 2-3 minutes.
- Mix in tomatoes, turmeric and salt. Sauté well, till oil rises to the surface and tinda are cooked.
- Sprinkle in coriander leaves and cook for a minute more.
- Remove from heat and serve.

Cook's tip: Choose tinda that have fine 'hair' on the skin, as these are the tender ones.

ALOO-SHIMLA MIRCH

Sautéed Potato and Capsicum

Serves: 4

2 large potatoes

2 large capsicums

2 tbsp oil

1/2 tsp black pepper powder

3/4 tsp salt

1 tsp mango powder (aamchur)

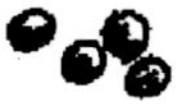

- Wash potatoes and cook under pressure for 5 minutes. Peel when cool, cut into eight pieces each and set aside.
- De-seed capsicums and cut into 2" pieces.
- Place oil in a kadhai over medium heat, till just beginning to smoke.
- Add capsicums, black pepper, salt and mango powder.
- As capsicums soften, after 4-5 minutes, put in potatoes. Stir over medium heat for a few minutes. Sprinkle a few drops of water if it tends to stick.

MASALA KARELA

Spicy Bitter Gourd

Serves: 4

250 gms bitter gourd (karela)

2 tbsp oil

1 large onion, finely sliced

1 tsp salt

1 tbsp coriander powder

2 tsp aniseed (saunf), dry-ground

1 tsp turmeric powder

$^1/_2$ tsp red chilli powder

$^1/_2$ tsp garam masala powder

$^1/_2$ tsp mango powder (aamchur)

- Trim ends of bitter gourds. Halve them lengthwise and then breadthwise. Cut each piece into $^1/_2$" thick slices.
- Place oil in a kadhai over medium heat, till just beginning to smoke.
- Add onion and fry till brown, stirring frequently. Lower heat, if it appears to be burning.
- Mix in bitter gourds and sauté for 2-3 minutes.
- Sprinkle in salt, coriander, aniseed and turmeric, and sauté over low heat, stirring constantly, till bitter gourds are cooked. You may sprinkle in a little water if the spices start to burn.
- Just before removing from heat, add remaining spices and sauté for a minute.
- This dish goes well with a dal and roti.

BITTER GOURD AND POTATO MASH

Serves: 4

This is a standard first course to a Bengali meal, as it is believed that something bitter ought to be eaten everyday to cleanse the system. It is always seasoned with raw mustard oil.

2 tender bitter gourds (karela), without seeds

1 medium potato

1 tbsp mustard oil

1/2 tsp salt

1 green chilli, broken into bits

- Wash vegetables and cook under pressure for 3-4 minutes.
- Open cooker after it has cooled.
- Drain vegetables. Peel potato and trim the ends of bitter gourds.
- Mix all ingredients with your hands, mashing the mixture to make a smooth paste.
- Serve with rice at the start of the meal.

Variation: Boiled vegetables mashed with mustard oil, salt and green chillies is a common side dish in eastern India. You can prepare potatoes, red pumpkin, yam (zimikand), wax gourd (parval) and ridge gourd (tori) in the same way.

SAUTÉED BITTER GOURD

Serves: 4

250 gms bitter gourd (karela)

Tempering

1 tbsp oil

2 whole dried red chillies, tops broken

1/2 tsp mustard seeds

10-15 curry leaves

- Wash bitter gourds and cook under pressure for 2 minutes.
- Drain, trim the ends and slice into 1/2" thick rounds.
- Place oil for tempering in a kadhai over medium heat, till just beginning to smoke.
- Add red chillies and fry till they darken slightly.
- Sprinkle in mustard seeds and when they start to sputter add curry leaves.
- Immediately add bitter gourds, and sauté for 2-3 minutes.
- Serve hot.

MASALA BAINGAN

Spicy Baby Aubergines

Serves: 4

500 gms small aubergines (baingan)

2 tbsp oil

Pinch of powdered asafoetida (hing)

2 tsp coriander powder

1 tsp cumin powder

1/2 tsp red chilli powder

1/2 tsp turmeric powder

1 tsp mango powder (aamchur)

1 tsp salt

- Wash aubergines and slit lengthwise at the base, leaving them intact with the stalks on.
- Place oil in a frying pan or kadhai over medium heat, till just beginning to smoke.
- Add asafoetida and almost immediately add aubergines. Sauté for 3-4 minutes over medium heat.
- Sprinkle in spice powders except mango powder, and stir well. Lower heat, cover pan and cook, stirring occasionally till aubergines are almost done.
- Stir in mango powder and salt, and cook for another minute for the dish to be ready.

BAINGAN BHARTA

Mashed Roasted Aubergine

Serves: 4

1 large round aubergine (baingan), about 500 gms

1 tbsp mustard oil, or more, according to taste

1 medium onion, finely chopped

2 green chillies, chopped (optional)

2 tsp chopped coriander leaves

1/2 tsp salt

- Slit aubergine down the centre, keeping stalk end intact. Discard if you find any worms in it.
- Lightly coat the skin with mustard oil. Place on a hot tava and cover with a deep pan, to retain heat.
- Roast over medium heat for 15 minutes turning it 3-4 times, to cook evenly on all sides.
- Pierce with a fork or long knife. If it goes in with no effort, it is ready.
- Allow to cool and peel.
- Mash with remaining ingredients and serve hot.

BAINGAN BHARTA – WITH EGG

Mashed Roasted Aubergine with Egg

Serves: 4

1 large round aubergine (baingan), about 500 gms

1 tbsp mustard oil

4 tbsp oil

1 medium onion, finely chopped

1 tsp finely chopped ginger

1 tsp finely chopped garlic

1 tsp red chilli powder (optional)

1 tsp garam masala powder

3 eggs

1 tsp salt

Garnish
2 tbsp chopped coriander leaves

- Slit aubergine and coat with mustard oil.
- Roast and peel as described in previous recipe.
- Place oil in a kadhai or frying pan over medium heat, till just beginning to smoke.
- Add onion and fry till pink, stirring frequently. Lower heat, if it appears to be burning.
- Add ginger and garlic, and fry for a minute over high heat.
- Lower heat and sprinkle in chilli powder (if used) and garam masala. Cook for 2 minutes, stirring constantly.
- Add aubergine and mash it in.
- Beat eggs lightly with salt and 2 tbsp water.
- Stir it slowly into the bharta and keep stirring over low heat till eggs have coagulated.
- Serve garnished with coriander leaves.

Variation: Stir in a tablespoon of crushed dried fenugreek leaves (kasuri methi) with the ginger and garlic. Do not use coriander garnish.

SAUTÉED CAULIFLOWER AND POTATO

Serves: 4

1 medium cauliflower, (about 500 gms)

2 medium potatoes

1 tsp salt

Tempering
1 tbsp oil

2 green chillies, tops broken

1/2 tsp panch-phoran or nigella seeds (kalaunji)

- Cut cauliflower into florets and wash. Peel potatoes, cut into halves and cut each half into 4 slices.
- Place oil in a kadhai over medium heat, till just beginning to smoke.
- Add green chillies and sauté for 5-10 seconds.
- Sprinkle in panch-phoran or nigella seeds and sauté for 5 seconds.
- Stir in vegetables and sauté for 3-4 minutes over high heat.
- Add salt and 1 cup water. Mix well, lower heat and cook covered, stirring once in a while till water is absorbed and vegetables are cooked.

Cook's tip: The cauliflower tastes good if left a bit underdone. To do this, cut them larger than the potatoes.

Variations: You may even skip the potatoes altogether and cook only cauliflower using this recipe.

Add 1/4 cup shelled green peas for colour.

CRUNCHY FRIED OKRA

Serves: 4

500 gms tender okra (bhindi)

1/2 tsp salt

1 tsp turmeric powder

1 cup oil

- Wash okra and dry thoroughly. Trim and cut into fine rounds.
- Toss okra in salt and turmeric, and keep aside.
- Place oil in a frying pan or small kadhai over medium heat, till just beginning to smoke.
- Using a slotted spoon, put in a batch of okra and fry till crisp and brown, stirring occasionally.
- Drain and place on a newspaper or paper towel spread out on a plate to absorb the oil.
- Repeat frying in batches, till all the okra are fried.
- Serve immediately or they will lose their crispness.

Variation: Okra fried like this make a delicious raita, when mixed into whipped curd. Mix just before serving or it becomes limp.

MASALA BHINDI

Spicy Okra

Serves: 4

Punjabis make a lovely version of okra stuffed with dry powdered spices. Instead of stuffing the okra, you can take a short cut and just sauté them with the same spices. The taste is equally good.

500 gms tender okra (bhindi)

3 tbsp oil

1/2 tsp ajwain

3 tsp cumin powder

2 tsp coriander powder

1 tsp red chilli powder

1 tsp mango powder (aamchur)

- Wash okra and dry thoroughly. Trim the ends and keep okra whole.
- Place oil in a frying pan or kadhai over medium heat, till just beginning to smoke.
- Add ajwain and fry for 5-10 seconds.
- Lower heat, add remaining spices except mango powder, and stir-fry for 10 seconds taking care not to burn them.
- Add okra and continue to stir-fry over low heat till they are cooked.
- Add mango powder and stir till okra are well coated with the spices.
- Remove from heat and serve hot.

TORAN

French Beans with Coconut

Serves: 6

500 gms French beans, trimmed and finely chopped

$^1/_2$ fresh coconut, grated

1 small onion, finely chopped

2-3 green chillies, slit lengthwise

1 tsp salt

Tempering

1 tbsp oil

$^1/_2$ tsp mustard seeds

10-15 curry leaves

- Combine beans, coconut, onion, green chillies and salt, and set aside.
- Place oil over medium heat in a heavy-bottomed kadhai, which has a lid of its size, till just beginning to smoke.
- Sprinkle in mustard seeds and when they start to sputter, add curry leaves.
- Immediately add bean mixture and cover kadhai. Cook for 2 minutes over high heat.
- Open kadhai, stir, cover again and cook for another 3 minutes over medium heat.
- Check if cooked yet crunchy, and serve.

Variation: Finely chopped cabbage or bitter gourd (karela) may be cooked in the same way. Discard bitter gourd seeds if they are too hard. The addition of the coconut tones down the bitterness of the vegetable and the resulting dish is delicious.

SOOKHI ARVI

Sautéed Colocasia

Serves: 4

500 gms colocasia (arvi)

4 tbsp oil

1/2 tsp ajwain

1/2 tsp salt

1/2 tsp turmeric powder

- Wash colocasia well and place in a pressure cooker with 1 cup water. Close cooker and place over high heat. Remove from heat when it starts hissing (Do not let the cooker reach full pressure and whistle, or the colocasia gets overdone and slimy.)
- Immediately place cooker under running cold water to cool, and open it.
- Peel colocasia as you would peel boiled potatoes and slit each in half lengthwise.
- Place oil in a large non-stick frying pan over medium heat, till just beginning to smoke.
- Add ajwain and when it starts to sputter, add colocasia, salt and turmeric.
- Stir well to coat colocasia and sauté over medium heat till brown and crisp on all sides. This may take a little time, so you have to be patient to get it right.

STIR-FRIED CABBAGE

Serves: 4

1 medium cabbage, (about 500 gms)

2 tbsp oil

2 whole dried red chillies, tops broken

1/2 tsp husked black lentils (urad dal)

1/2 tsp mustard seeds

1/2 tsp finely chopped ginger

1 medium onion, finely chopped

10-15 curry leaves

1 tsp salt

- Cut cabbage into quarters and slice each quarter finely.
- Place oil in a kadhai over medium heat, till just beginning to smoke.
- Add red chillies and urad dal, and fry till dal turns light brown.
- Sprinkle in mustard seeds and when they start to sputter, add ginger, onion and curry leaves. Fry over medium heat till onion is light pink, stirring frequently. Lower heat, if it appears to be burning.
- Add cabbage and salt, stir well to mix, lower heat and cover kadhai with a lid.
- Let cabbage cook in its own steam for 8-10 minutes, stirring occasionally so that it doesn't burn. Sprinkle in some water, if it appears to dry up before it is done.

STIR-FRIED RADISH

Serves: 4-6

2 medium white radishes with tender leaves (they should not be prickly)

1/2 tsp salt

Tempering

2 tbsp oil

2 whole dried red chillies, tops broken

1/2 tsp mustard seeds

- Wash and scrape radishes. Chop radishes and leaves separately.
- Place oil for tempering in a kadhai over medium heat, till just beginning to smoke.
- Add red chillies and mustard seeds.
- When mustard seeds start to sputter, add radish. Stir over medium heat for 2-3 minutes till radish softens.
- Add radish leaves and stir for a few moments. Add salt, cover and lower heat.
- After 2 minutes uncover kadhai and stir till just done and the liquid dries out.

STIR-FRIED CARROTS

Serves: 4

4-5 medium carrots (about 250 gms)

1/2 tsp salt

3 green chillies, slit or 1/2 tsp red chilli powder (optional)

1 tbsp chopped coriander leaves

Tempering
2 tbsp oil

1/2 tsp cumin seeds or nigella seeds (kalaunji)

- Peel and cut carrots into 1/4" thick rounds.
- Place oil for tempering in a pan over medium heat, till just beginning to smoke.
- Add cumin or nigella seeds.
- When they start to sputter, add carrots, salt and green chillies or chilli powder. Stir-fry over medium heat for about 10 minutes, till just done. If you fry beyond this, the carrots will get too soft.
- Add coriander leaves, stir for a minute and serve.

Cook's tip: The cumin and nigella seeds each give a different flavour.

ALOO-KASURI METHI

Potatoes with Fenugreek

Serves: 4

This is a convenient dish that dispenses with the bother of cleaning fresh fenugreek greens. It uses dried fenugreek leaves which can be bought packaged from most grocery stores.

2 large potatoes

1/2 tsp salt

Tempering
2 tbsp oil

4 whole dried red chillies, tops broken

2 tbsp dried fenugreek leaves (kasuri methi)

- Wash potatoes and cook under pressure for 5 minutes.
- Cool, peel, cut into 2" cubes and set aside.
- Place oil in a kadhai over medium heat, till just beginning to smoke.
- Add red chillies and fry till they darken slightly.
- Lower heat and sprinkle in fenugreek leaves. Fry for 3-4 seconds, ensuring that they do not burn.
- Add potatoes and salt, raise heat to medium and sauté, stirring for a few minutes till well coated in spices.

TOSSED POTATOES AND GREEN PEAS

Serves: 4-6

This dish is literally, as the name suggests, boiled green peas and potatoes, lightly tossed in a little butter and spices. It's quick to make and poori, paratha or roti make a good accompaniment.

6 medium potatoes

1 cup shelled green peas, fresh or frozen

1/2 tsp + 1/2 tsp salt

1/2 tsp black pepper powder, preferably freshly ground

Tempering

1 tsp oil

1 tsp butter or ghee

1/2 tsp nigella seeds (kalaunji)

- Wash potatoes and pressure-cook for 3 minutes.
- Cool, peel and cut into 2" cubes.
- Boil green peas in an open pan with 1/2 tsp salt for 3-4 minutes till just done, but bright green. Drain and set aside.
- Place oil and butter or ghee in a heavy-bottomed kadhai over medium heat, till butter or ghee has just melted.
- Rub nigella seeds between your palms to enhance their flavour, sprinkle into kadhai and fry for 10 seconds.
- Add potatoes and green peas and raise heat to high. Add pepper and 1/2 tsp salt, and stir briskly till vegetables are evenly coated with the spices.
- Remove from heat and serve hot.

CHORCHORI

Mixed Vegetables

Serves: 4-6

A Bengali dish, chorchori is made with different combinations of vegetables, depending on family favourites. No spices are used except for a panch-phoran tempering, which subtly adds to the natural flavours of the vegetables.

2 medium potatoes

200 gms red pumpkin (kaddu)

1 medium aubergine (baingan)

1 small cauliflower (about 250 gms)

1/2 cup shelled green peas

1 tsp salt

Tempering
1 tbsp oil

2 green chillies, tops broken

1/2 tsp panch-phoran

- Peel potatoes and pumpkin. Cut potatoes, pumpkin and aubergine into 2" pieces. Break cauliflower into small florets.
- Place oil for tempering in a kadhai over medium heat, till just beginning to smoke.
- Add green chillies and fry for a few moments.
- Sprinkle in panch-phoran and sauté for 15 seconds.
- Add vegetables and raise heat. (If you do not like hot food, remove green chillies at this stage.) Stir-fry vegetables for around 3 minutes.
- Add salt and 1 cup water. Cover kadhai and cook over medium heat, till the vegetables are tender, for about 10 minutes.
- The liquid should dry out for the dish to be ready.

Variation: You can susbstitute any of the vegetables with French beans, sheet beans (saem phalli), carrots, radish or whole spinach leaves.

POTATO AND ONION CURRY

Serves: 4

This is a quick and simple curry that tastes delicious with roti or poori and could also be served for brunch.

4 large potatoes

2 tbsp oil

4 whole green chillies, tops broken

2 large onions, sliced

1 tsp turmeric powder

1 tsp salt

- Peel and wash potatoes, cut into thick round slices and then into vertical strips.
- Place oil in a kadhai over medium heat, till just beginning to smoke.
- Add green chillies and fry for 10 seconds.
- Add onions and sauté till pink, stirring frequently. Lower heat if they appear to burn.
- Stir in potatoes, turmeric and salt, and continue to stir for 1-2 minutes.
- Pour in 2 cups water and boil over high heat till potatoes are done and you have a thin gravy.

GREEN PUMPKIN AND RAW MANGO

Serves: 4

500 gms green-skinned pumpkin (kaddu)

1 medium, unripe mango or 1 tsp mango powder (aamchur)

1/2 tsp turmeric powder

1/2 tsp salt

2-3 green chillies, slit

Tempering

1 tbsp oil

Pinch of powdered asafoetida (hing)

1/2 tsp fenugreek (methi) or mustard seeds

- Grate pumpkin along with its skin.
- Peel and grate mango (if used) and keep aside.
- Place oil for tempering in a kadhai over medium heat, till just beginning to smoke.
- Sprinkle in asafoetida and fenugreek or mustard seeds, and when they start to sputter add pumpkin, turmeric and salt.
- Cook uncovered over high heat stirring occasionally. The pumpkin will let off a lot of water and will cook quite fast.
- When the liquid is almost dry, add grated mango or mango powder and green chillies. Stir well to mix thoroughly.
- Remove from heat when the liquid has dried out.

MUSHROOMS SAUTÉED IN BUTTER

Serves: 4

People often overlook this dish because of its simplicity. But, the less spice added to mushrooms the better the natural flavour. This dish can be served as an accompaniment with eggs, or just served on buttered toast, or even as a side dish with a spicy meat preparation.

1 packet (200 gms) button mushrooms

1 tbsp butter

1/4 tsp salt

1/2 tsp black pepper powder

- Wash mushrooms and cut in half.
- Melt butter in a frying pan or kadhai over low heat and add mushrooms.
- Season with salt and pepper, raise heat to high and sauté for 5 minutes.

Cook's tip: For added flavour, you may add 1/2 tsp dried herbs like parsley, basil, or oregano, or experiment with your favourite ones.

LAUKI KALAUNJI

Bottle Gourd with Nigella

Serves: 4

750 gms bottle gourd (lauki)

1/4 tsp turmeric powder

1/2 tsp salt

Tempering
1 tbsp oil

1/4 tsp nigella seeds (kalaunji)

2 green chillies, tops broken

Garnish
2 tbsp chopped coriander leaves

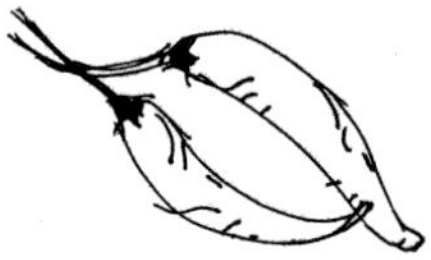

- Peel bottle gourd and cut into fine juliennes.
- Place oil for tempering in a kadhai over medium heat, till just beginning to smoke.
- Rub nigella between your palms to enhance their flavour and add with green chillies.
- When nigella seeds start to sputter, put in the bottle gourd, turmeric and salt.
- Raise heat to high and stir-fry for 3-4 minutes.
- Lower heat and cook covered for 10-15 minutes.
- Check once in a while to ensure that it has not dried out. If necessary sprinkle in a little water.
- Remove from heat when bottle gourd is cooked, garnish with coriander leaves and serve.

LAUKI HING-JEERA

Sautéed Bottle Gourd

Serves: 4-6

750 gms bottle gourd (lauki)

1/2 tsp red chilli powder

1/2 tsp turmeric powder

1 tsp coriander powder

1/2 tsp salt

1 tsp mango powder (aamchur)

Tempering
2 tbsp oil

Pinch of powdered asafoetida (hing)

1/2 tsp cumin seeds

- Peel and cut bottle gourd into 1/2" cubes.
- Combine spice powders except mango powder with 1 tbsp water to make a paste.
- Place oil for tempering in a kadhai over medium heat, till just beginning to smoke.
- Sprinkle in asafoetida and cumin seeds.
- When cumin seeds start to sputter, stir in spice paste and stir-fry for about 30 seconds.
- Add bottle gourd and salt, and continue to stir-fry over medium heat for 3-4 minutes.
- Lower heat, cover pan and cook till done, stirring occasionally.
- Stir in mango powder and cook for a minute more.
- This dish is meant to be semi-dry and cooks without the addition of any water. If it tends to dry up too much, sprinkle in a little water, so that it does not burn.

Cook's tip: To choose a tender bottle gourd, the skin should be firm but easily pierced by the nail.

RED PUMPKIN AND POTATO

Serves: 4

250 gms red pumpkin (kaddu)

2 medium potatoes

1 tbsp coriander powder

1/2 tsp turmeric powder

1/2 tsp red chilli powder

1 tsp salt

Tempering

2 tbsp oil

2 whole dried red chillies, tops broken

Pinch of powdered asafoetida (hing)

1/2 tsp panch-phoran

- Peel pumpkin and potatoes, and cut into 1" cubes.
- Place oil for tempering in a kadhai over medium heat, till just beginning to smoke.
- Add red chillies and asafoetida.
- After 3-4 seconds, add panch-phoran and when the seeds start to sputter, mix in vegetables.
- Sauté over high heat for 3-4 minutes, stirring all the time.
- Stir in spice powders, salt and 1 cup water.
- Cover kadhai, lower heat to medium and cook for 10-15 minutes, checking occasionally to see that the water has not dried out. Sprinkle in about 1/2 cup water, if necessary.
- When cooked the pumpkin should be very soft and the potatoes just done.
- The dish should be moist, but not watery.

paneer, soya, tofu

Paneer, soya nuggets, and tofu (soya bean curd) are a rich source of protein for vegetarians. They are also a tasty substitute for meat or chicken, when cooking a vegetarian meal. Paneer is readily available at dairies and can also be made at home, soya nuggets are sold at grocers, while tofu is available at shops that stock Chinese ingredients.

TOFU IN SOY SAUCE

Serves: 4

250 gms tofu (bean curd)

1/2 tsp finely chopped ginger

1/2 tsp finely chopped garlic

1/2 tsp black pepper powder

4 tbsp soy sauce

- Cut tofu into 2" squares and arrange in a flat baking dish.
- Sprinkle ginger, garlic, pepper and soy sauce over tofu.
- Cover dish with foil and bake in an oven preheated to 180°C (350°F) for 20 minutes.
- Alternately you can steam it (see p. xxx).
- Serve hot with plain rice or Chinese fried rice.

TOFU, CABBAGE AND MUSHROOMS

Serves: 4-6

250 gms tofu (bean curd)

500 gms cabbage

4 tbsp oil

1/2 tsp finely chopped ginger

1/2 tsp finely chopped garlic

1 packet (200 gms) button mushrooms, halved

2 spring onions with greens, chopped

1 chicken or vegetable stock cube

2 tsp cornflour

1/2 tsp salt

1/2 tsp black pepper powder

2 tbsp soy sauce

- Cut tofu into 2" squares.
- Separate cabbage leaves. Cut off the thick middle vein of each leaf with a sharp knife.
- Place oil in a large frying pan or kadhai over medium heat, till just beginning to smoke.
- Add cabbage, ginger and garlic, and sauté for 2 minutes.
- Stir in tofu, mushrooms and spring onions.
- Dissolve stock cube in 1 cup hot water and pour into pan.
- Mix cornflour with 1/4 cup cold water and stir it in.
- Add salt, pepper and soy sauce, and simmer for 5 minutes, till gravy thickens, stirring continuously.
- Serve with plain rice or Chinese fried rice.

PANEER MAKHANI

Cottage Cheese in Tomato Gravy

Serves: 4-6

This dish could be a vegetarian substitute for murgh makhani. The butter naturally adds to the taste and makes it a rich dish. But you could very well cook a lighter version with oil if you want to cut down on calories.

500 gms cottage cheese (paneer)

50 gms butter

1 tsp ginger-garlic paste

1 large onion, grated

1 packet (200 gms) tomato purée

1 tsp salt

Garnish
2 tbsp chopped coriander leaves or dried fenugreek leaves (kasuri methi)

- Cut paneer into thin, flat slices, about 2" square and 1/2" thick.
- Place butter in a kadhai over medium heat till melted.
- Stir in ginger-garlic paste and sauté for 15 seconds.
- Add onion and sauté for 2 minutes, stirring frequently till pink.
- Pour in tomato purée and fry for 3-4 minutes over high heat.
- Add paneer and salt, and simmer covered for 10 minutes.
- Garnish with coriander leaves or crushed dried fenugreek leaves and serve hot.

Cook's tip: Use 2 tbsp oil in place of butter if you like.

PANEER BHURJI

Scrambled Cottage Cheese

Serves: 4-6

500 gms cottage cheese (paneer)

1/2 cup shelled green peas (optional)

2 tbsp oil

1/2 tsp cumin seeds

1 large onion, finely chopped

1 tsp ginger-garlic paste

1/2 tsp turmeric powder

1/2 tsp salt

1/2 tsp garam masala powder

1 tsp dried fenugreek leaves (kasuri methi) – optional

Garnish
2 tbsp chopped coriander leaves

- Crumble paneer coarsely.
- Boil green peas (if used) in salted water.
- Place oil in a pan over medium heat, till just beginning to smoke.
- Add cumin seeds and when they start to sputter, add onion and ginger-garlic paste. Sauté till onion turns pink, stirring frequently.
- Stir in paneer, green peas (if used), turmeric and salt. Sauté till the moisture in the paneer dries up.
- Sprinkle in garam masala and dried fenugreek leaves (if used) and cook for another minute.
- Remove from heat and garnish with coriander leaves.

CHANA PANEER

Chickpeas with Cottage Cheese

Serves: 4-6

1 cup chickpeas (kabuli chana) or husked Bengal gram (chana dal)

250 gms cottage cheese (paneer)

3 tbsp oil

1 large onion, grated or ground in the mixer

1 tsp ginger-garlic paste

2 tbsp chopped coriander leaves

1 tsp salt

2 tsp coriander powder

1 tsp turmeric powder

1 tsp cumin powder

1/2-1 tsp red chilli powder

2 medium tomatoes, chopped

1 tsp garam masala powder

- Soak chickpeas (if used) overnight and rinse. There is no need to soak chana dal.
- Cook chickpeas or dal with 3 cups water under pressure for 10 minutes.
- Cut paneer into 1" cubes.
- Place oil in a frying pan or kadhai over medium heat, till just beginning to smoke.
- Fry paneer in 2-3 batches, till lightly browned. Drain and set aside.
- In the same oil fry onion and ginger-garlic paste for 2-3 minutes, stirring frequently.
- Add coriander leaves, salt and spice powders except garam masala, and sauté for 30 seconds.
- Stir in tomatoes and sauté till oil rises to the surface.
- Pour in boiled chickpeas or chana with the cooking liquid and simmer till you have a thick gravy.
- Add paneer and garam masala, simmer for 2-3 minutes and remove from heat.

BOTTLE GOURD WITH SOYA NUGGETS

Serves: 4-6

1 1/2 cups soya nuggets

750 gms bottle gourd (lauki)

1 tsp chilli powder

1 tsp coriander powder

2 tbsp oil

1 tsp ginger paste

1 tsp garlic paste

2 tbsp onion paste

1 large tomato, finely chopped

1 tsp salt

Garnish
1 tbsp chopped coriander leaves

- Soak soya nuggets in boiling water for 5 minutes and drain.
- Peel and cut bottle gourd into 1" cubes.
- Mix chilli and coriander powders with 1 tbsp water.
- Place oil in a kadhai over medium heat till just beginning to smoke.
- Add ginger, garlic and onion, and fry till pink.
- Stir in chilli-coriander paste and tomatoes.
- Fry till tomatoes are cooked and the mixture turns brown.
- Add bottle gourd and salt. Raise heat and stir for 3-4 minutes.
- Add soya nuggets and stir for 2-3 minutes further.
- Add 2 cups water (or as required) and simmer till bottle gourd is cooked.
- Serve garnished with chopped coriander leaves.

SWEET 'N SOUR SOYA NUGGETS

Serves: 4-6

2 cups soya nuggets

2 large onions

1 large capsicum

2 tbsp oil

1/2 packet (100 gms) tomato purée

1/4 cup malt vinegar (optional)

2 tbsp soy sauce

2 green chillies, chopped

1 tsp sugar

1 tsp salt

- Soak soya nuggets in boiling water for 5 minutes. Drain and set aside.
- Cut onions into quarters and separate the layers.
- Cut capsicum into 2" pieces and discard seeds.
- Place oil in a frying pan over medium heat, till just beginning to smoke.
- Add onions and capsicum, and sauté over high heat for 2 minutes, stirring all the while.
- Stir in remaining ingredients except soya nuggets and sauté for a minute.
- Add soya nuggets and stir well so that they soak up the gravy. Add 1/2 cup water if the nuggets appear too dry. Cook for 2-3 minutes and remove from heat.
- Serve with plain rice or Chinese fried rice.

Cook's tip: You can make the same dish using 250 gms paneer cubes instead of soya nuggets. Just skip the first step.

eggs

Eggs are the most versatile ingredient for quick no-fuss cooking and they can be combined with almost anything to make a complete meal. They can enhance the flavour of boring vegetables (Parsis cook eggs with okra, fenugreek leaves, etc.). They can be used for thickening gravies, or be stirred into leftovers to increase the quantity. However, it is important that you buy eggs fresh and refrigerate them, as they do not last long in Indian weather. Eggs with discoloured or broken yolks should be avoided.

EGGS IN MUSTARD GRAVY

Serves: 6

6 hard-boiled eggs

2 tbsp black or yellow mustard seeds, dry-ground

1/2 tsp turmeric powder

1/2 tsp salt

2 tbsp oil

3-4 whole green chillies, tops broken

2 medium onions, sliced

Garnish
1/2 tbsp chopped coriander leaves

- Shell eggs and cut lengthwise into halves.
- Make a paste with ground mustard seeds, turmeric, salt and 1/2 cup water.
- Place oil in a frying pan over medium heat, till just beginning to smoke.
- Add green chillies and fry for a few seconds.
- Add onions and fry till pink, stirring frequently.
- Gently slip in eggs. Pour mustard paste over them and simmer over low heat for 5 minutes.
- Turn eggs gently with a flat spatula, taking care not to separate the yolks and whites.
- Cook for another 3 minutes, checking to see that the gravy does not stick at the base of the pan. Sprinkle in some water if needed.
- Garnish with coriander leaves and serve hot.

DHABA BHURJI

Scrambled Eggs – Indian-style

Serves: 4-6

This is a rough-and-ready bhurji that makes a lovely brunch with hot paratha or roti.

3 tbsp oil

1 tsp dried fenugreek leaves (kasuri methi) – optional, but it enhances the taste

1/2 tsp ginger paste

1/2 tsp garlic paste

2 green chillies, chopped

1 large onion, chopped

1/2 tsp turmeric powder

1/2 tsp red chilli powder

1/2 tsp salt

6 eggs

Garnish
2 tbsp chopped coriander leaves

- Place oil in a frying pan or kadhai over medium heat, till just beginning to smoke.
- Add fenugreek leaves, ginger, garlic and green chillies, and fry for a minute.
- Add onion and fry till light pink, stirring frequently.
- Sprinkle in turmeric, chilli powder and salt, and fry for 30 seconds.
- Quickly break in the eggs one at a time. Stir vigorously over high heat till eggs scramble and spices are evenly distributed.
- Garnish with coriander leaves and serve hot.

SPICY EGGS WITH ONIONS

Serves: 6

6 hard-boiled eggs

3 tbsp oil

4 large onions, finely sliced

1 tsp red chilli powder

1/2 tsp salt

Garnish
2 tbsp chopped coriander leaves

- Shell and cut eggs lengthwise into halves or quarters.
- Place oil in a large pan over medium heat, till just beginning to smoke.
- Add onions and fry till light brown, stirring frequently. Lower heat, if they appear to be burning.
- Add chilli powder and salt, and continue to fry for 30 seconds more.
- Add eggs and stir gently, till well coated with spices; for less than a minute.
- Serve garnished with coriander leaves.

SAUTÉED EGGS AND POTATOES

Serves: 4

4 eggs (at room temperature)

2 medium potatoes

2 tbsp oil

1/2 tsp cumin seeds

1" stick cinnamon

2 green cardamoms

4 cloves

1/2 tsp salt

- Wash eggs and potatoes and place them in a pressure cooker with enough water to cover. Cook under pressure for 4-5 minutes.
- Shell and cut eggs lengthwise into quarters.
- Peel and cut potatoes into cubes.
- Place oil in a frying pan or kadhai over medium heat, till just beginning to smoke.
- Add cumin seeds and whole spices, and fry for 10-15 seconds.
- Add potatoes, eggs and salt, and gently toss together till well mixed.
- Serve hot.

Cook's tip: Eggs can be cooked in a pressure cooker—alone or with potatoes—for dishes where the eggs have to be boiled in advance. Just see to it that the eggs are at room temperature and the shells are washed clean.

EGG-DROP CURRY

Serves: 4-6

This is a simplified version of the traditional egg curry where the eggs are boiled first. Here they are broken into the curry directly.

2 tbsp oil

2 bay leaves

1" stick cinnamon

2 green cardamoms

3 cloves

2 tsp ginger-garlic paste

1 large onion, grated or finely chopped

1 tbsp coriander powder

1 tsp cumin powder

1/2 tsp turmeric powder

1/2 tsp chilli powder

1 tsp salt

2 medium tomatoes, chopped

4-6 eggs

Garnish
Chopped coriander leaves

- Place oil in a frying pan or kadhai over medium heat, till just beginning to smoke.
- Add bay leaves and whole spices, and almost immediately add ginger-garlic paste. Sauté for 15 seconds.
- Add onion and sauté till light brown.
- Stir in spice powders, salt and tomatoes, stir well and fry till the oil comes to the surface.
- Pour in 4 cups water and bring to boil. Continue boiling over high heat for 2 minutes.
- Break each egg gently into the bubbling gravy. The eggs will soon set. Continue to boil over high heat for 5 minutes more.
- Serve garnished with chopped coriander leaves.

PLAIN OMELETTE

Serves: 1

2 eggs

1 tbsp milk

1 tbsp chopped onions

1 tsp chopped coriander leaves or fresh parsley

1 tbsp butter

Salt and pepper to taste

- Beat eggs with milk briskly for about a minute.
- Stir in onion and coriander leaves or parsley.
- Heat butter over low heat, in an 8" frying pan, till it just foams.
- Gently pour in egg mixture and raise heat to medium. As the mixture sets, push the edges towards the centre with a wooden spatula, creating an empty space, and tilt the pan so that the remaining liquid flows into it and sets.
- Repeat this process till the entire omelette is set. It should be golden at the base and soft and moist on top.
- Sprinkle with salt and pepper, fold in half and serve with a salad.

Cook's tip: Omelettes are best fried in a small frying pan, about 8" in diameter. Keep a separate non-stick frying pan of this size, just for your eggs if you eat them often.

Variation: ***Chinese Omelette****: Beat eggs in a bowl briskly for about a minute. Stir in 1/2 tsp each of finely chopped ginger and garlic, 1 tsp each of chopped coriander leaves and soy sauce, 1/4 tsp pepper and a pinch of salt, and cook and serve as above.*

SPANISH OMELETTE

Serves: 4

2 tbsp oil

1 large onion, sliced in rings

1 large potato, peeled and sliced in thin rounds

1/2 tsp salt

1/2 tsp black pepper powder

1 tbsp fresh, chopped or 1 tsp dried herbs such as parsley, basil, oregano

4 eggs

- Place oil in a medium-sized, non-stick frying pan over medium heat, till just beginning to smoke.
- Add onion and potato, and fry over high to medium heat. Instead of stirring, hold frying pan by the handle and swirl contents around occasionally. Cook till onions and potatoes are golden.
- Add salt, pepper and herbs, and sauté for 10 seconds.
- Break eggs into a bowl, whisk well and pour into the pan over the vegetables.
- Lower heat and cook till the eggs set over the vegetables. If the top has not set, cover pan for a few moments.
- The omelette should be golden brown around the edges.
- Cut into 4 wedges and serve hot with bread of your choice.

fish

A Chinese chef once advised us that truly fresh fish should smell of the fresh sea breeze. In fact, the fish we buy shouldn't really smell fishy, because if it does, it isn't fresh! Look out for certain sure signs of freshness when buying fish: the scales should shine, the stomach should be firm and not depressed, the eyes should be glistening and not sunken, and the gills should be bright red especially in the case of river fish.

RATNAGIRI FISH CURRY

Serves: 6

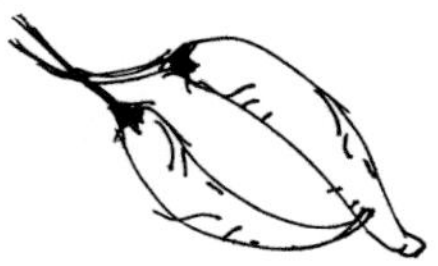

500 gms sea fish like surmai, sole or pomfret, cut into 2" cubes

1/2 fresh coconut, ground **(see p. 10)**

1 tbsp coriander powder

1 tsp red chilli powder

1 tsp turmeric powder

1 tsp garam masala powder (preferably the Maharashtrian variety)

1 tbsp tamarind paste or 5-6 pieces of kokum

2 cups water

1 tbsp oil

Ground together

1 whole garlic

1" piece ginger

1 medium onion

- Wash fish well and drain.
- Mix all the ingredients in a deep pan or kadhai that has a lid.
- Place pan on heat and gently bring to boil.
- Stir gently, taking care not to break fish pieces.
- Cover and simmer over low heat for 10 minutes.
- Serve hot, preferably with rice.

DAHI MACHH

Fish in a Curd-based Gravy

Serves: 6

500 gms rohu or katla, preferably from a large fish, cut into 1" thick pieces (steaks)

1/4 tsp turmeric powder

1/2 tsp + 1/2 tsp salt

3 tbsp oil

1/2 tsp panch-phoran

4 whole dried red chillies, tops broken

1 tbsp ginger paste

2 cups curd, drained

1 tsp sugar (optional)

Garnish
10-15 sultanas (kishmish) – optional

- Wash fish, rub with turmeric and 1/2 tsp salt and set aside.
- Place oil in a non-stick frying pan over medium heat, till just beginning to smoke.
- Add panch-phoran, red chillies and ginger, and fry for 30 seconds.
- Add fish and sauté lightly on both sides till the flesh whitens.
- Beat curd well with sugar and remaining salt, and pour over fish.
- Cook over very low heat for around 10 minutes. The curd will curdle if you cook it over high heat. Turn the fish once during the process, scraping the base lightly if the curd sticks.
- Garnish with sultanas (if used).

KERALA FISH CURRY

Serves: 6

500 gms fillets or 2" cubes of mackerel, black pomfret, surmai or sole

3 tbsp oil

1/2 tsp mustard seeds

1/4 tsp fenugreek seeds (methi)

2 medium onions, sliced

1" piece ginger, finely chopped

5-6 cloves garlic, finely chopped

1 tsp turmeric powder

1 tbsp red chilli powder

1 tbsp coriander powder

1 tsp salt

3-4 sprigs curry leaves

2 tsp tamarind pulp or 5-6 pieces kokum

2 medium tomatoes, chopped

Garnish

6 green chillies, slit lengthwise

- Wash fish well and set aside to drain.
- Place oil in a kadhai over medium heat, till just beginning to smoke.
- Sprinkle in mustard and fenugreek seeds.
- When they start to sputter, add onions, ginger and garlic, and sauté till light brown, stirring frequently. Lower heat if it appears to be burning.
- Add spice powders, salt and curry leaves, and fry for 30 seconds.
- Stir in tamarind or kokum and tomatoes, and cook slowly for 5 minutes till oil rises to the surface.
- Pour in about 3-4 cups water to make a gravy and bring to boil.
- Slip in fish and simmer for 15 minutes.
- Garnish with green chillies and serve with rice.

Cook's tip: This fish curry improves in flavour if refrigerated and served a day after cooking it.

Note: Kokum is the dried fruit of the gamboge (garcina) tree. It is used as a souring agent and is available in most grocery shops.

MACHCHI KALAUNJI

Fish with Nigella Seeds

Serves: 6

2 medium potatoes

500 gms rohu, katla or pomfret, cut into 1" thick pieces (steaks)

1/2 tsp + 1/2 tsp turmeric powder

1/2 tsp + 1 tsp salt

1/4 cup oil

3 whole green chillies, tops broken

1/2 tsp nigella seeds (kalaunji)

1" piece ginger, finely chopped

1 large onion, sliced

2 tbsp chopped coriander leaves

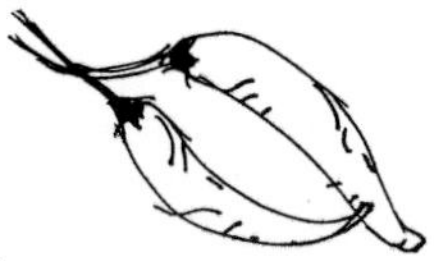

- Peel potatoes and cut lengthwise into 6 pieces each.
- Wash fish and coat with 1/2 tsp turmeric and 1/2 tsp salt.
- Place oil in a kadhai over high heat, till just beginning to smoke.
- Gently slip in fish and fry lightly for about a minute on each side. Keep the heat high, or the fish will stick to the kadhai. Remove fish from kadhai, drain and set aside.
- Lower heat to medium, add green chillies and fry for about 30 seconds.
- Rub nigella seeds between your palms to enhance their flavour and sprinkle in.
- Almost immediately, add ginger and onion, and fry till onion is pale pink, stirring frequently.
- Add potatoes and sauté for 2 minutes.
- Sprinkle in remaining salt and turmeric, and pour in about 4 cups water.
- Bring to boil and add fish. Lower heat to medium and cook uncovered till potatoes are done. There should be plenty of thin gravy.
- Stir in coriander leaves and remove from heat.

CHINGRI MACCHER MALAI CURRY

Prawns in Coconut Sauce

Serves: 6

This classic Bengali dish gets its name from its Malaysian influence.

1 kg tiger or jumbo prawns, preferably with the heads on, cleaned and de-veined

1/2 tsp turmeric powder

1/2 tsp + 1/2 tsp salt

3 tbsp oil

2 bay leaves (tej patta)

4 green cardamoms

4 cloves

4 x 1/2" sticks cinnamon

1 large onion, grated or ground to a paste

1 tsp ginger paste

1 tsp garlic paste

1 tsp red chilli powder

2 cups thick coconut milk (see p. xx)

- Rub turmeric and 1/2 tsp salt into prawns and set aside.
- Place oil in a kadhai over medium heat, till just beginning to smoke.
- Toss in bay leaves and whole spices, and sauté for 10 seconds.
- Stir in onion, ginger and garlic, and sauté for about 5 minutes till light brown, stirring frequently. Lower heat if it appears to be burning.
- Sprinkle in chilli powder and 1/2 tsp salt.
- Add prawns and sauté for 3-4 minutes, till the flesh turns firm and opaque.
- Pour in coconut milk and simmer over low heat for 5 minutes.
- Serve hot with rice.

BIHAR FISH CURRY

Serves: 6

Don't get intimidated by the grinding of the spices. It's the only hassle in this extremely tasty fish curry.

500 gms rohu or katla, cut into 1" thick pieces (steaks)

1/2 tsp + 1/2 tsp turmeric powder

1/2 tsp + 1 tsp salt

3 tbsp poppy seeds

1 tbsp mustard seeds

10 cloves garlic

1 tsp cumin powder

1 tsp red chilli powder

1/4 cup oil, preferably mustard oil

2 medium, ripe tomatoes, chopped

Garnish
2 tbsp chopped coriander leaves

- Rub fish with 1/2 tsp turmeric and 1/2 tsp salt and set aside.
- Dry-grind poppy and mustard seeds in the grinder. Add garlic and cumin and chilli powders with a little water and grind to a thick paste.
- Place oil in a kadhai over high heat, till just beginning to smoke. Gently slip in fish and fry lightly for about a minute on each side. Keep the heat high, or the fish will stick to the kadhai. Remove fish, drain and set aside.
- Add ground masala paste to kadhai and sauté till oil rises to the surface.
- Stir in tomatoes, remaining turmeric and salt and continue frying till oil rises to the surface.
- Add 2 cups water and bring to boil. Slip fish into gravy and cook over low heat for 10 minutes.
- Garnish with coriander leaves.

BAKED FISH WITH TOMATO

Serves: 6

500 gms fillets of any firm-fleshed fish like bhetki, pomfret, surmai or tuna

1 tsp salt

1 tsp ginger-garlic paste

8-10 medium, ripe tomatoes (500 gms), cut in round slices

3-4 medium onions, cut in rings

4 tbsp chopped coriander leaves or fresh parsley

4 x 1" sticks cinnamon

6 cloves

10-15 black peppercorns

2 bay leaves (tej patta)

- Wash fish well and rub with salt and ginger-garlic paste.
- In a flat baking dish arrange 1/3 of the tomatoes, onions and coriander leaves or parsley in a layer. Arrange half the fish over this.
- Scatter half the whole spices and a bay leaf over the fish.
- Arrange another layer of vegetables, followed by a layer of fish. Scatter over the remaining whole spices and bay leaf, and cover with remaining vegetables.
- Bake uncovered in an oven preheated to 200°C (400°F) for 30 minutes.

FRIED FISH

Serves: 6

Use any of the marinades given below to prepare fried fish.

500 gms rohu, singhara, pomfret, seer, tuna or mackerel, filleted or cut into pieces

1/2 cup oil

Marinade-1

Juice of 2 limes

2" piece ginger, grated

1 heaped tsp black pepper powder

1/2 tsp turmeric powder

1/2 tsp salt

Marinade-2

Juice of 2 limes

2 tsp ginger-garlic paste

2 tsp sambar masala powder

1/2 tsp turmeric powder

1/2 tsp salt

Marinade-3

2 tsp tamarind pulp

1 tsp garlic paste

1 tsp red chilli powder

- Combine ingredients for any marinade of your choice. Wash fish, drain and rub in marinade.
- Allow fish to marinate for 30 minutes to 2 hours.
- Place oil in a deep frying pan or kadhai over high heat, till just beginning to smoke. Slip in fish in batches and fry each side over high heat for 2 minutes.
- Lower heat to medium and fry each side for a further 3-5 minutes, depending on the thickness of the pieces, till fish is cooked through and evenly browned.

chicken

Another easily and widely available meat in India; the choice varies from selectively fed, farm-bred broilers to your around-the-corner murgiwallah who may even sell desi free-range chicken. In the North or down the Gangetic plain till Orissa, you will only find chicken without skin, unless you go to a cold storage. Such birds are freely available but buy them from a reliable butcher. If buying chicken with skin, look for a plump bird with a healthy pink colour. Avoid slow-moving cold storage outlets and don't buy large or old birds. Free-range chicken taste better, but take twice the time to cook.

FRIED CHICKEN

Serves: 4-8

8 chicken legs (drumsticks)

1/2 tsp + 1/2 tsp salt

1/2 tsp black pepper powder

1 cup flour (maida)

1 tsp baking powder

2 eggs

2/3 cup milk

1 tsp oil

Oil for deep-frying

- Wash chicken legs, drain and sprinkle with 1/2 tsp salt and pepper.
- Sift flour, baking powder and 1/2 tsp salt in a large bowl and set aside.
- Beat eggs till fluffy, add milk and 1 tsp oil and beat again. Stir in flour lightly to make a batter. Do not beat too much.
- Place oil for deep-frying in a frying pan or kadhai over medium heat, till just beginning to smoke. Coat chicken legs evenly in batter and fry 3-4 pieces at a time. When chicken is golden, reduce heat and fry for 6-8 minutes till cooked through. Remove from oil, drain and place on kitchen paper to absorb excess oil.

BUTTER CHICKEN

Serves: 6

1 chicken (about 1 kg), jointed

2 tsp + 50 gms butter

2 tbsp onion paste

1 tsp garlic paste

1 tsp ginger paste

1 packet (200 gms) tomato purée

1 tsp Kashmiri chilli powder

1 tsp salt

1 tsp dry fenugreek leaves (kasuri methi)

- Wash chicken well and set aside to drain.
- Melt 2 tsp butter in a kadhai over medium heat.
- Add onion, garlic and ginger, and fry for 2 minutes.
- Add chicken and 50 gms butter, and sauté over medium heat for 5 minutes.
- Add tomato puree, chilli powder and salt, and sauté further for 2-3 minutes.
- Pour in enough water to cover chicken completely and simmer covered for 10-15 minutes till chicken is tender.
- Stir in fenugreek leaves and remove from heat.
- Serve hot with added butter on top if desired.

PARSI CHICKEN CURRY WITH STRAW POTATOES

Serves: 6

1 chicken (about 1 kg), jointed

2 tbsp oil

2 large onions, finely sliced

2 medium tomatoes, chopped

1 tsp salt

3 whole green chillies, tops broken

100 gms straw potatoes (juliennes of potato, fried crisp, also known as salli or lachha)

Ground to a smooth paste

10 cloves garlic

3 whole dried red chillies, de-seeded if you don't want it hot

2 tsp cumin seeds

- Wash chicken well and set aside to drain.
- Place oil in a kadhai over medium heat, till just beginning to smoke. Add onions and fry till golden brown, stirring frequently. Lower heat if they appear to be burning.
- Add chicken, ground spices, tomatoes and salt. Sauté over medium heat, till chicken is well browned, adding a little water when required, to prevent spices from burning.
- Pour in 2 cups water and add green chillies. Stir well and cook covered over low heat for 20-25 minutes, till chicken is tender and gravy is thick.
- When ready to serve, reheat chicken and spoon onto a flat platter. Sprinkle over straw potatoes and serve.

Cook's tip: Don't sprinkle the straw potatoes over chicken in advance or they will get soggy.

COQ AU VIN

Chicken in Wine

Serves: 6-8

1 chicken (about 1 kg) preferably with skin, cut into 8-10 pieces

200 gms bacon, coarsely chopped

2 tbsp oil

1 large onion, sliced

5 cloves garlic, chopped

2 carrots, cut into 2" pieces

1 tbsp mixed herbs like basil, oregano, thyme and rosemary

2" stick cinnamon

15 black peppercorns

1 tsp salt

2 cups red or white wine

1 packet (200 gms) button mushrooms

- Wash chicken well and set aside to drain.
- Heat a kadhai or large frying pan till medium-hot, add bacon and fry without oil till crisp. Remove bacon and set aside.
- Add oil to bacon fat left in the kadhai or frying pan and heat till just beginning to smoke.
- Add chicken, fry over medium heat till golden brown, remove and set aside.
- Add onion and garlic, and fry till onion is light brown, stirring frequently. Lower heat if it appears to be burning.
- Add carrots, herbs, whole spices, salt and 2 cups water.
- Bring to boil, add chicken, bacon, wine and mushrooms, lower heat and simmer for 20-25 minutes till chicken is done.

Cook's tip: Go easy with the salt as the bacon is highly salted. Use 1/2 packet (100 gms) tomato purée instead of wine if your kitchen is a dry area, though the taste will not be the same.

STIR-FRIED CHICKEN

Serves: 6

500 gms boneless chicken, cut into 1" cubes

1 tbsp + 2 tbsp oil

2 large onions, sliced into rings

Marinade

1 tsp salt

1 tsp coarsely ground black pepper

1/2 tsp garlic paste

Juice of 4 limes

Garnish

2 tbsp chopped coriander leaves

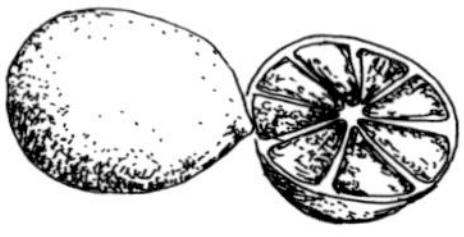

- Wash chicken well and set aside to drain.
- Combine ingredients for marinade, rub into chicken and marinate for 2 hours, stirring it a few times.
- Heat 1 tbsp oil in a kadhai over high heat and swirl kadhai around to coat the surface evenly.
- Add chicken and stir-fry over high heat for 8-10 minutes. It should be just cooked. Pinch out a bit of flesh from a piece and taste to check. Remove from kadhai and set aside.
- Heat 2 tbsp oil in the kadhai, over medium heat till just beginning to smoke.
- Add onions and fry till light brown, stirring frequently. Lower heat if they appear to be burning.
- Add chicken, stir for a minute and place in a serving dish. Garnish with coriander leaves and serve.

EVERYDAY CHICKEN CURRY

Serves: 6

1 chicken (about 1 kg), jointed

3 tbsp oil

2" stick cinnamon

3-4 black cardamoms

1 tsp ginger paste

1½ tsp garlic paste

2 medium onions, sliced

2 tbsp coriander powder

1 tsp turmeric powder

1 tsp red chilli powder

1 tsp salt

2 tbsp malt vinegar or sour curd

- Wash chicken well and set aside to drain.
- Place oil in a pressure cooker over medium heat, till just beginning to smoke.
- Toss in whole spices and fry for 10 seconds.
- Stir in ginger and garlic, and brown lightly for 30 seconds.
- Add onions and sauté till golden, stirring frequently. Lower heat if they appear to be burning.
- Mix in spice powders, salt and vinegar or curd, and sauté for 2 minutes.
- Add chicken and sauté for 2-3 minutes till well coated with the spices.
- Pour in 2 cups water, close cooker and cook under pressure for 4-5 minutes.

PAN-FRIED CHICKEN

Serves: 6

1 large chicken (about $1\frac{1}{4}$ kg) preferably with skin, jointed

$\frac{1}{2}$ tsp crushed mace flakes (optional)

1" stick cinnamon

6 cloves

10 black peppercorns

1 tsp red chilli powder

$\frac{1}{2}$ tsp garlic paste

$\frac{1}{2}$ tsp ginger paste

1 cup curd

1 tsp salt

4 tbsp oil

Garnish
2-3 onions, sliced in rings and fried crisp (optional)

- Wash chicken well and set aside to drain.
- Dry-grind mace, cinnamon, cloves and peppercorns to a coarse powder.
- Mix with chilli powder, garlic, ginger, curd and salt. Marinate the chicken in this mixture for over 6 hours on the lower shelf of the refrigerator.
- Place oil in a large non-stick frying pan over high heat, till just beginning to smoke.
- Add as many chicken pieces as fit into the pan. Brown chicken on all sides for a minute to seal in the juices.
- Lower heat to medium-low, cover pan and cook each side of chicken for 5 minutes. Drain and place on a paper towel to absorb excess oil. Fry the next batch in the same way.
- Serve hot, garnished with onion rings (if used).

CHILLI CHICKEN

Serves: 8

1 kg chicken with bone, cut into bite-sized pieces

2 tbsp oil

1 cup chopped spring onions, with greens

2 tbsp chopped green chillies, de-seeded if you want it less hot

Marinade

1/2 tsp garlic paste

1/2 tsp ginger paste

1/4 cup soy sauce

2 tbsp malt vinegar

- Wash chicken well and set aside to drain.
- Combine ingredients for marinade, rub into chicken and marinate for 6 hours or more.
- Cook chicken in its marinade in a covered pan over low heat for 20 minutes, till just done. No water needs to be added. The chicken will release a lot of its own fluids, but if it dries up, add a little water.
- Alternatively, you may cook it under pressure for 2 minutes. Drain chicken and set aside.
- To serve, place oil in a large kadhai over high heat, till just beginning to smoke.
- Add spring onions and green chillies, and stir-fry over high heat for a minute. Add chicken, stir well and serve immediately.

Cook's tip: This dish is usually served dry. If you like a bit of gravy add some stock. Avoid salt as soy sauce has lots of it.

BURMESE KHOUSWE

Serves: 6-8

This may seem complicated, but is quite easy to make. Khouswe includes a curry, several garnishes and noodles. The garnishes are the most interesting part of the dish. We give you a few essentials here, but use your imagination and as you gain the khouswe-experience, add anything that tickles your palate. It makes a lovely single dish for a party.

1 broiler chicken with skin (1-1 1/2 kg)

2 tbsp oil

1 tsp turmeric powder

1 tbsp ginger paste

1 tbsp garlic paste

2 tbsp onion paste

1 heaped tsp salt

1 tsp black pepper powder

1 tsp Thai fish paste or 2 tbsp Thai fish sauce (adds a distinct flavour, but not essential; if you are using this ingredient, reduce the salt to 1 level tsp)

3 cups thick coconut milk

Chicken curry

- Wash chicken well and set aside to drain.
- Cook chicken with 1 cup water in a pressure cooker placed over high heat. Remove from heat when cooker reaches full pressure (first whistle). Cool, debone chicken and set aside meat.
- Pressure cook bones again in 2 cups water for 10 minutes to make some more stock. Cool and strain stock. Discard bones.
- Place oil in a kadhai over medium heat, till just beginning to smoke. Add turmeric, ginger, garlic and onion, and stir-fry till onion begins to brown. Lower heat if it appears to be burning.
- Add chicken, salt and pepper, and stir for a few minutes.
- Add fish paste or sauce to 1 cup hot stock. If using fish paste, stir well to ensure that it dissolves.
- Add to chicken and keep stirring to blend well. Stir in remaining stock and bring to boil.
- Pour in 1 cup water and as the mixture simmers, lower heat and slowly pour in coconut milk. Let the mixture simmer over low heat for a few minutes and set aside.

Garnishes

20 cloves garlic, chopped

4 small onions, finely sliced

10 whole dried red chillies

10 green chillies

200 gms small frozen shrimps

3 limes

4 hard-boiled eggs

2 spring onions

A bunch of coriander leaves

Noodles

500 gms noodles

1 tbsp oil

Garnishes

- Prepare each ingredients as given, place in individual bowls and serve separately.
- Fry garlic till brown in a little oil and drain.
- Fry onions till brown in the same oil, stirring frequently. Lower heat if they appear to be burning. Drain.
- Dry roast red chillies on a tava, ensuring they do not burn and crush into coarse flakes.
- Chop green chillies fine. De-seed them first if you don't want it too hot.
- Boil shrimps and chop fine.
- Cut limes into quarters to squeeze over the curry.
- Grate eggs, or chop very fine.
- Chop spring onions fine.
- Chop coriander leaves fine.

Noodles

- Cook noodles in plenty of salted boiling water for the time specified on the packet.
- Drain in a colander and rinse under running cold water.
- Pour out into a serving dish, drizzle over oil, and toss.

To serve

- Serve curry and noodles in separate serving dishes and arrange garnishes around them.
- For individual helpings, first take some noodles in a soup bowl and spoon in the chicken curry over it. Sprinkle the garnishes in the combination you prefer.

mutton

Mutton means goat's meat in India, as opposed to the West, where it means sheep's meat. It is the most widely acceptable meat in all communities. As a rule, go for a younger animal that is not too thin nor too fat. The meat should look red and smell fresh. Refrigerated meat takes on a pallid white or pink hue. For curries use the legs, preferably the hind legs. Chops, breast, neck or the back have higher bone content and unless you specify your cut to the butcher, you will usually end up with more bones than meat.

KEEMA MATAR

Mince with Green Peas

Serves: 4

250 gms mince

3 tbsp oil

2 tbsp onion paste

1 tsp ginger paste

1 tsp garlic paste

2 tsp coriander powder

1 tsp black pepper powder

1 tsp garam masala powder

1 cup shelled peas

1 tsp salt

Garnish
1 tbsp chopped coriander leaves

- Pressure-cook mince with 1/2 cup water for 5 minutes and set aside.
- Place oil in a kadhai over medium heat, till just beginning to smoke. Add onion and stir-fry till it turns pink. Add ginger and garlic, and fry for about 4 minutes.
- Add coriander powder and fry for another 2 minutes on medium heat. Sprinkle in pepper and garam masala, and fry for 4 minutes further. If the spices show signs of sticking to the sides, splash in a few drops of water.
- Drain mince and reserve stock. Add mince to the masala and mix well. Raise heat and stir-fry for 2 minutes.
- Add green peas, salt and stock, and simmer for 5 minutes over medium heat.
- Serve garnished with coriander leaves.

ALOO-GOSHT

Mutton and Potato Curry

Serves: 4

500 gms mutton with bone, preferably leg or shoulder, cubed

4 large potatoes

4 tbsp oil

3 tbsp onion paste

1 tsp ginger paste

1 tsp garlic paste

3 tsp coriander powder

1 tsp red chilli powder

2 tsp garam masala powder

1/2 cup curd

1 1/2 tsp salt

Garnish
2 tbsp chopped coriander leaves

- Wash mutton and set aside to drain.
- Cook potatoes under pressure with 2 cups water for 2 minutes. Cool, peel and cut into 4 or 6 pieces each.
- Cook mutton under pressure with 1 cup water for 10 minutes. Set aside to cool.
- Place oil in a large kadhai over medium heat, till just beginning to smoke. Add onion and fry till it starts to redden, stirring frequently. Lower heat if it appears to be burning.
- Add ginger and garlic, and fry for a few minutes further. Sprinkle in coriander powder and stir-fry over medium heat till mixture is brown and oil starts to separate. If it tends to stick to the sides or burn, sprinkle in a little water. Mix chilli and garam masala powders with curd, beat well and add. Stir over medium heat till curd and spices are well blended.
- Strain mutton and reserve stock. Raise heat, add mutton to masala and stir-fry over high heat for 5 minutes. Lower heat, add potatoes and keep stirring as mutton and potatoes get coated with the spices and dry out.
- Add stock and salt, raise heat, adjust liquid in the curry to your requirement by adding water and bring to boil. Lower heat and simmer for 10 minutes. Garnish with coriander and serve.

MASOOR-GOSHT

Red Lentils with Mutton

Serves: 4-6

1 cup masoor, whole or husked

500 gms mutton with bone, cubed

2 tbsp ghee

2 medium tomatoes, finely chopped

1 tsp salt

Mixed together
4 tbsp onion paste

1 tsp garlic paste

2 tbsp ginger paste

1 tsp turmeric powder

1 tsp red chilli powder

2 tsp coriander powder

1 tsp cumin powder

1 tsp garam masala powder

Garnish
1 tbsp chopped coriander leaves

- Clean and wash dal and set aside to soak in water for 30 minutes.
- Pressure-cook mutton with 2 cups water for 10 minutes. Strain out mutton and reserve stock.
- Place ghee in cooker over medium heat, till just melted and fry spice-paste till brown, ensuring it does not burn. Sprinkle in a little water, if necessary.
- Add tomatoes and fry till well blended. Sprinkle in a few drops of water if necessary.
- Add mutton and stir for a few minutes.
- Add salt, dal and reserved stock with enough water to cover by 2". Cook under pressure for 5 minutes. Open cooker after it has cooled.
- Serve garnished with coriander leaves.

Cook's tip: This dish goes well with roti, rice or hot crusty buns and makes a satisfying winter meal.

SPAGHETTI BOLOGNAISE

Serves: 4-6

Always cook your sauce before the pasta. Then just before serving, cook the pasta fresh (you will have to take this trouble), mix in the warmed-up sauce with the hot pasta and serve. You may even make the sauce in advance, keep it in the refrigerator and reheat before serving.

2 tbsp olive oil, or any other oil

1 large onion, finely chopped

10 cloves garlic, chopped

500 gms mince

1 stick celery, finely chopped (optional)

10 button mushrooms, halved and finely sliced

1/2 tsp black pepper powder

1/2 tsp grated nutmeg

1 tsp dried basil or oregano

1 tsp + 2 tsp salt

1 packet (200 gms) tomato purée

1/2 cup red wine (optional, but adds dramatically to the flavour)

1 packet (400 gms) spaghetti or tagliatelle

Bolognaise sauce

- Place oil in a pan over medium heat, till just beginning to smoke. Add onion and garlic and sauté till onion turns pink, stirring frequently. Lower heat if it appears to be burning.
- Add mince, celery and mushrooms, and sauté over high heat till all the moisture evaporates.
- Sprinkle in pepper, nutmeg, herbs and 1 tsp salt, and sauté for 15 seconds.
- Pour in tomato purée and wine (if used), and cook, stirring till it is reduced to half and the raw smell of the tomato goes away.

Pasta

- Bring 2 litres water to boil in a large pan. Add 2 tsp salt and pasta. Cook, stirring occasionally for 6-10 minutes, or according to the instructions on the packet.
- Taste a strand to see if it is al dente—a bit underdone. If it needs more boiling, stand by the stove and cook a little longer. Pasta left unattended always gets overdone.

4 tbsp fresh Parmesan cheese or any processed cheese, grated

- Drain pasta in a colander, shaking it to get all the water out.
- Serve as soon as the pasta is ready, in individual plates or a serving dish, with the sauce poured over it and grated cheese sprinkled on top.

Variation: Use chopped breakfast sausages in place of mince.

Cook's tip: For the authentic taste, blanch 1/2 kg ripe tomatoes in boiling water for 2 minutes, peel, chop and use in place of tomato purée.

AJWAIN LIVER-FRY

Serves: 6

500 gms liver, cubed

2 tbsp oil

1/2 tsp salt

Marinade

2 tsp ginger-garlic paste

3 tsp ajwain, dry-ground

1 tsp red chilli powder

1/2 cup thick curd or juice of 2 limes

- Wash liver and drain.
- Combine ingredients for marinade, rub into liver and marinate for 30 minutes.
- Place oil in a non-stick frying pan over high heat, till just beginning to smoke.
- Add marinated liver and salt, and fry over high heat for about 5 minutes till liquid evaporates. Do not over-cook the liver as that makes it tough.
- Serve with French fries and browned onion rings (optional).

MUTTON POT ROAST

Serves: 4-6

1-1 1/2 kg whole leg of mutton

1 1/2 tsp garlic paste

1 1/2 tsp ginger paste

Juice of two limes or 1/4 cup malt vinegar

1 tsp black pepper powder

1 tsp salt

2 tbsp oil

Dry-ground together
1/2 tsp crushed mace flakes

2" stick cinnamon

8 cloves

- Wash and dry mutton. Score it with a sharp knife making diagonal cuts, 2" apart and about 1" deep.
- Mix ground spices with garlic, ginger, lime juice or vinegar, pepper and salt. Rub the mixture well all over the leg, ensuring that it enters the scored parts.
- Cover and leave overnight on a lower shelf of the refrigerator. You can marinate it for up to 36 hours. In fact the longer it is kept the better.
- Keep turning it every 5-6 hours, so that the joint remains well marinated on all sides and the juices do not drain out from one side.
- Place oil in a large frying pan or kadhai over high heat, till just beginning to smoke. Gently slip the leg into the pan, reserving the residual marinade. Keep a cover handy, as it will sputter.
- Fry over high heat, turning frequently, so that it browns evenly without burning.
- Lower heat, add reserved marinade and fry for another 6 minutes, turning frequently.
- Transfer contents of pan to a pressure cooker. Add 1/2 cup water and pressure-cook for 15 minutes. Open cooker after it has cooled.
- Serve hot or cold, slicing it at the table or before bringing it out, if you prefer.

SPICY MACARONI WITH MINCE

Serves: 6

1 cup macaroni

3 tbsp oil

2 bay leaves (tej patta)

2 medium onions, chopped

2 tsp ginger-garlic paste

1 large tomato, chopped

1 tsp salt

2 tsp coriander powder

1 tsp turmeric powder

$^{1}/_{2}$-1 tsp red chilli powder

1 tsp garam masala powder

500 gms mince

Garnish

2 tbsp chopped coriander leaves

- Cook macaroni till al dente (see Spaghetti Bolognaise p. 118) and set aside.
- Place oil in a kadhai over medium heat, till just beginning to smoke.
- Add bay leaves and onions, and fry till onions are light brown, stirring frequently. Lower heat if they appear to be burning.
- Add ginger-garlic paste and fry for 30 seconds.
- Stir in tomato, salt and spice powders, and cook till the oil rises to the surface.
- Add mince and fry for 2-3 minutes.
- Pour in 1 cup water and cook over medium heat for 5 minutes.
- Add macaroni and adjust the gravy, which should be thick, with more water if needed.
- Boil for 2-3 minutes and garnish with coriander leaves before serving.
- Serve with rice, roti or paratha, but not as a pasta dish in itself.

ROGHAN JOSH

Serves: 6

1 kg mutton with bone, cubed

4 tbsp oil

1/4 tsp powdered asafoetida (hing)

2 x 1" sticks cinnamon

4 green cardamoms

4 cloves

2 tsp ginger paste or 1 tsp powder (saunth)

4 tsp aniseed (saunf), dry-ground

2 tsp coriander powder

2 tsp Kashmiri chilli powder

2 cups thick curd

1 tsp salt

- Wash mutton and set aside to drain.
- Place oil in a pressure cooker over medium heat, till just beginning to smoke.
- Add asafoetida and whole spices, and sauté for 10 seconds.
- Raise heat to high and add mutton. Fry over high heat for 5-6 minutes till mutton turns brown.
- Add ginger and spice powders, and sauté for a minute.
- Stir in 2 tbsp curd. Sauté for 2-3 minutes till the water dries up and add 2 tbsp more of curd. Continue with this process till the curd is used up, mutton is well browned and the oil has risen to the surface.
- Add salt and 3 cups water, and cook under pressure for 7 minutes.

KERALA MUTTON-FRY

Serves: 6

This makes an excellent snack with drinks or can be served as a main dish. The dish tastes good made with beef as well.

1 kg boneless mutton, cut into 2" pieces

3 tbsp oil

2 large onions, sliced

Marinade

1 tsp garam masala powder

4 tsp aniseed (saunf), dry-ground

1/2 tsp black pepper powder

1 tsp red chilli powder

1 tsp turmeric powder

1 tsp salt

2 tsp ginger-garlic paste

3 tbsp malt vinegar

- Wash meat and drain.
- Combine ingredients for marinade, rub into meat and marinate for an hour.
- Place meat and marinade in a pressure cooker with 1/2 cup water. Cook under pressure for 5 minutes.
- Place oil in a large non-stick frying pan over medium heat, till just beginning to smoke.
- Add onions and fry till brown, stirring frequently. Lower heat if they appear to be burning.
- Pour in contents of pressure cooker and fry over high heat till all the moisture dries up.
- Tastes excellent served with French fries.

pork

Pork is one of the most delicious meats and can be cooked in any style. It is not widely popular in India because of certain cultural associations and the unhygienic conditions in which pigs are reared. However, there are traditional farms, and some new ones, where they are reared according to the strictest norms of animal husbandry. So it is important that you find out where to buy safe pork. Most large cities always have a safe shop or two and you can ask some pork lover about their whereabouts. Indian pork also comes with inordinately large amounts of fat and it makes sense buying it fatless. For the recipes in this book, meat from the hindlegs would be the best suited.

PORK CHOPS

Serves: 4

4 pork chops, about 200 gms each

2 tbsp oil

1 small onion, grated

Marinade
1 tsp ginger-garlic paste

2 tbsp Worcestershire sauce

1 tbsp soy sauce

$^1/_2$ tsp salt

$^1/_2$ tsp black pepper powder

1 tsp dried herbs of your choice like basil, oregano or thyme

- Wash chops and pat dry with a clean cloth.
- Combine ingredients for marinade and marinate chops for 1-2 hours.
- Place oil in a pressure cooker over medium heat, till just beginning to smoke.
- Add onion and fry till brown, stirring frequently. Lower heat if it appears to be burning.
- Add chops and sauté for 3-4 minutes.
- Pour in $^1/_4$ cup water and pressure cook chops for 15 minutes.

BACON AND MIXED VEGETABLE STEW

Serves: 4-6

This is a lovely meal to rustle up on a cold evening. Nothing can be more pleasurable in winter than mopping up a steaming stew from an enormous bowl with fresh crusty bread.

250 gm solid chunk of bacon (slices will also do)

2 tbsp butter

2 bay leaves (tej patta)

10 black peppercorns

2 medium onions, sliced

6 cloves garlic, crushed

4 tbsp flour (maida)

2 medium carrots, peeled and cut into 2" pieces

1 small cauliflower, (250 gms), cut into florets

10 French beans, trimmed and cut into 2" pieces

10 button mushrooms

2 medium, ripe tomatoes, chopped

1/2 cup shelled green peas

- Cut bacon chunk into 1/2" cubes, or if using slices, cut into 2" strips.
- Have enough boiling water ready for adding to gravy.
- Heat butter in a heavy-bottomed pan or kadhai, till just melted and fry bacon over high heat till browned.
- Toss in bay leaves and peppercorns, and sauté for 30 seconds.
- Add onions and garlic, and sauté till light brown, stirring frequently. Lower heat if it appears to be burning.
- Reduce heat to low and stir in flour. Continue stirring till it is brown and exudes a roasted aroma.
- Add the remaining ingredients and cook, stirring for 5 minutes.
- Pour in enough hot water to cover bacon and vegetables by 1".

1/2 tsp dried thyme

1 tsp dried tarragon (optional)

1 tsp salt

- Bring to boil, lower heat, cover pan and simmer till vegetables are done.
- Adjust gravy with hot water according to your taste and cook for a few more minutes.
- Remove from heat and serve piping hot with fresh crusty bread.

Cook's tip: If you add cold water to the stew, the flour will form lumps.

PORK MAKHA

Pork and Potato Hash

Serves: 4

This amazingly easy, yet tasty dish is cooked in Tripura and other parts of the North-east. 'Makha' means mixed.

500 gms pork, cut into pieces, with fat

4 medium potatoes, peeled and quartered

2 medium onions, chopped

2" piece ginger, julienned

4-5 green chillies, chopped (de-seeded if you don't want it too hot)

2 tbsp chopped coriander leaves

1 tsp salt

- Wash pork well and drain.
- Place pork, potatoes and half the onions and ginger in a pressure cooker with 1 cup water.
- Cook under pressure for 15 minutes.
- Open cooker after it has cooled.
- Heat through just before serving, stir in remaining ingredients and serve hot.

Cook's tip: You can add 2 tbsp mustard oil to enhance the flavour, as they do in Tripura.

PORK VINDALOO

Serves: 6

1 kg pork, cut into 2" cubes

1 tsp salt

1 tsp sugar

2 tbsp oil

2 large onions, finely chopped

Ground to a paste

10-15 dried red chillies, broken in half with the seeds shaken out

20 black peppercorns

8 cloves

2" stick cinnamon

2 tsp cumin seeds

1 tsp mustard seeds, yellow or black

10 cloves garlic

2" piece ginger

1/2 tsp turmeric powder

1/2 cup malt vinegar

- Wash pork and drain.
- Mix ground paste with salt and sugar, stir in pork and marinade for 2 hours or more. The longer it is marinated, the better it is.
- Place oil in a pressure cooker over medium heat, till just beginning to smoke.
- Add onions and sauté till light pink, stirring frequently. Lower heat if they appear to be burning.
- Add pork and sauté for 2-3 minutes.
- Stir in 2 cups water and cook under pressure for 20 minutes.

PINEAPPLE PORK

Serves: 4-6

1 kg boneless pork, without fat, cut into 1" cubes

6 whole dried red chillies

2 tbsp +1 tbsp oil

2 tbsp onion paste

2 tsp ginger paste

1 tsp garlic paste

1 tsp salt

1 cup spring onions with greens, cut into 1" pieces

2 leafy stems of celery, about 12" each, cut into 1" pieces

6 canned pineapple rings, cut into 6 pieces each

4-5 green chillies, chopped (optional)

- Wash pork well and place in a colander to drain for 30 minutes.
- Break red chillies in half and shake out the seeds, soak in a little less than 1/4 cup warm water and set aside.
- Place 2 tbsp oil in a pressure cooker over medium heat, till just beginning to smoke.
- Add onion and stir-fry for 2 minutes. Add ginger and garlic, and stir for another 2 minutes.
- Add pork and mix well. Fry over high heat for 5 minutes, stirring constantly.
- Swirl 1 cup water into the pressure cooker to wash the masala sticking to the sides. Stir in salt and pressure-cook for 10 minutes. Set aside to cool.
- Place 1 tbsp oil in a kadhai over medium heat, till just beginning to smoke. Add spring onions and celery, and stir-fry for a minute.
- Add pineapple and stir for 2 minutes.
- Pour in red chillies with soaking water and stir for another minute.
- Lower heat to medium, add pork and green chillies (if used), mix well and serve.
- The dish should be just moist.

desserts

A good meal is only complete with a satisfying dessert. However, making sweet-dishes seems to intimidate many amateur cooks (though some just specialise in fancy desserts and cannot cook anything else)! Desserts can be no-fuss too, and at the same time satisfy the most demanding sweet-tooth. We've delved into our collection to come up with the shortest and sweetest ones.

BHAPA DAHI

Indian Cheesecake

Serves: 8

2 cups hung curd made from 500 gms curd (see pg xx)

1 can (400 gms) condensed milk

Decoration
1 tbsp cashew nuts or almonds, coarsely chopped

1 tbsp sultanas (kishmish)

- Beat curd and condensed milk together till well blended and pour into a metal container that has a tight-fitting lid.
- Sprinkle over cashew nuts or almonds and sultanas and close the lid.
- Put 2 cups water in a pressure cooker, place the container in it and close cooker.
- Steam for 15 minutes without putting the weight on the pressure valve.
- Alternatively, you can steam it for 15 minutes in a rice cooker.
- Once you perfect the technique, you should be able to turn it out like a pudding on a plate. If you plan to do this, decorate with nuts and sultanas later.
- Chill, cut into wedges and serve.

SHRIKHAND

Serves: 6-8

4 cups (1 kg) fresh curd

1/2 cup powdered sugar

Powdered seeds of 2-3 green cardamoms

A few strands saffron soaked in 1 tsp milk (optional)

1 tbsp chopped pistachios (optional)

- Tie curd in a large, clean muslin cloth and hang it over the sink to drip for 5-6 hours. If you are doing this in summer, place curd in a large plastic strainer lined with muslin and keep it in the refrigerator with a bowl to catch the water below.
- Turn out curd into a clean glass bowl and beat in remaining ingredients.
- Serve chilled.

Cook's tip: The curd must be absolutely fresh. You cannot make this dish with curd that has gone even slightly sour.

Variation: Shrikhand can be served with fresh fruits such as grapes, strawberries, kiwi fruit and mango.

STRAWBERRY CHEESECAKE

Serves: 8-10

20 Marie biscuits

100 gm butter

4 cups curd, hung for 4-5 hrs (see p. xx)

1 cup condensed milk

2 heaped tsp gelatine, soaked in 4 tbsp lukewarm water

1 basket (200 gms) strawberries

- Put biscuits in a thick plastic bag and crush well with a rolling pin.
- Reserve 1 tsp butter and mix remaining butter with biscuit crumbs.
- Grease a round pudding dish with reserved butter and line with biscuit-butter mix. Place dish in the freezer for 15-20 minutes.
- Whisk curd, condensed milk, gelatine and half the strawberries (select the softer ones) in the liquidizer for a minute.
- Pour over biscuit base and freeze for 30 minutes or place in the refrigerator till set.
- Slice remaining strawberries and decorate top of cheesecake.
- Chill thoroughly, cut into wedges and serve.

LOW-FAT CHOCOLATE MOUSSE

Serves: 8

4 cups milk

6 tbsp cocoa powder

1/2 cup sugar

- Fill a large shallow pan or kadhai 1/3 with water and heat till simmering.

4 tbsp cornflour dissolved in $^1/_2$ cup cold milk

1 tsp vanilla essence

- Put milk into a smaller pan and place over simmering water to create a double boiler.
- Add cocoa and sugar, and keep stirring milk over simmering, not boiling, water.
- When bubbles appear at the edges of the milk, add cornflour mix and keep stirring till mousse thickens to a custard-like consistency.
- Remove from heat and cool.
- Stir in vanilla and pour mousse into individual dessert bowls or small glasses. Serve chilled.

Cook's tip: Heating the mousse indirectly gives it a smoother consistency.

SWEET VERMICELLI

Serves: 8

2 tsp + $^1/_2$ tsp ghee

2 cups thick vermicelli

A few strands saffron, soaked in water (optional)

1 cup sugar

Decoration

1 tbsp chopped cashew nuts

1 tbsp sultanas (kishmish)

- Heat 2 tsp ghee in a kadhai till it just melts and fry vermicelli till golden.
- Add saffron and 3 cups water, and cook till the water dries up.
- Add sugar and keep stirring till dissolved and remove from heat. At first the vermicelli will look soggy, but it dries up once you take it off the heat.
- Heat $^1/_2$ tsp ghee in a small frying pan and fry cashew nuts till golden-brown.
- Pour over vermicelli, sprinkle with sultanas and serve.

PHIRNI

Serves: 8

This classic Muslim dessert is extremely simple to make, yet quite impressive. It can even set without refrigeration, though it tastes better chilled.

4 tbsp rice

1 litre milk

1/3 cup sugar

1 tbsp kewra-water or 2-3 drops kewra essence

Decoration

1 tbsp pistachio slivers

Rose petals (optional)

- Wash rice, soak in water for 2-3 hours, drain and grind to a smooth paste in a liquidizer with a little water.
- Mix rice paste with milk, add sugar and bring to boil, stirring constantly so that no lumps are formed.
- Lower heat and simmer, still stirring till it takes on a thick custard-like consistency.
- Remove from heat and add kewra-water or essence.
- Pour into individual bowls and sprinkle over pistachio slivers and rose petals (if used).
- Once it cools put the bowls into the refrigerator (not freezer).
- The phirni will soon set and be ready to serve.

glossary

ENGLISH	HINDI
Almond	Badam
Aniseed	Saunf
Asafoetida	Hing
Aubergine	Baingan
Bay leaf	Tej patta
Bengal gram	
–flour	Besan
–husked	Chana dal
–whole	Kala chana
Black lentils	
–whole	Sabut urad
–husked	Urad dal
Black pepper	Kali mirch
Brinjal/Aubergine	Baingan
Cabbage	Band gobhi
Capsicum	Shimla mirch
Cardamom	
–black	Badi elaichi
–green	Hari / chhoti elaichi
Carom seeds	Ajwain
Carp	Rohu
Carrot	Gaajar
Cashew nut	Kaju
Cauliflower	Phool gobhi
Chickpeas	Kabuli / safed chana
Cinnamon	Dalchini / taj
Clove	Laung
Colocasia	Arvi
Coriander	
–fresh	Hara dhania
–seeds	Sabut dhania
Cottage cheese	Paneer
Cumin seeds	Jeera
Curd	Dahi
Curry leaf	Kari patta
Fenugreek	
–dry leaves	Kasuri methi
–fresh leaves	Methi saag
–seeds	Methi dana
French beans	Fransbin
Ginger	
–dry	Saunth
–fresh	Adrak
Gourd	
–bitter	Karela
–bottle	Ghia/Lauki
–ridge	Tori
Green lentils	
–husked	Moong dal
–whole	Sabut moong
Green peas	Mattar
Indian squash	Tinda
Kidney beans	Rajma
Lemon	Galgal

ENGLISH	HINDI
Lentils	Dal
Lettuce	Salad ke patté
Lime	Nimbu/limbu
Liver	Kaleji
Mace	Javitri
Mackerel	Bangda
Mango powder	Amchur
Mince	Keema
Mint	Pudina
Moong lentils	Moong dal
–husked	Dhuli moong
–whole	Sabut moong
Mushroom	Dhingri / khumbi
Mustard seeds	
–brown	Rai
–black	Sarson
–yellow	Peeli sarson
Nigella	Kalaunji
Nutmeg	Jaiphal
Okra/Lady's finger	Bhindi
Peppercorn	Kali mirch
Pigeon peas	Arhar / toover dal
Pistachio nuts	Pista
Poppy seeds	Khus khus
Prawn	Jhinga
Pumpkin	
–white	Doodhiya
–red / yellow	Seetaphal / kaddu
Radish	Mooli
Red lentils	Masoor dal
–husked	Dhuli masoor
–whole	Sabut masoor
Saffron	Kesar / Zafran
Screwpine flower essence	Kewra
Seer / Kingfish	Surmai
Sheet beans	Saem Phalli
Spinach	Palak
Spring onions	Hara pyaz
Sultana	Kishmish
Tamarind	Imli
Turmeric	Haldi
Vermicelli	Sevian
Vinegar	Sirka
Wheat	Gehun
–plain / refined flour	Maida
–whole wheat flour	Atta
Yoghurt/curd	dahi
Panch phoran	A Bengali spice mix made with five spices—onion seeds, aniseed, fenugreek seeds, mustard seeds and cumin seeds.